STAYING IN TUNE

STAYING IN TUNE

a *sane* response to your child's music

Al Menconi
with Dave Hart

Standard Publishing

This book was previously published under the title, *Today's Music: A Window to Your Child's Soul,* by David C. Cook Publishing Co. Many of the examples have been updated.

Edited by Dale Reeves
Assistant editor, Greg Holder
Design by settingPace
Cover Design by settingPace
Images © 1996 PhotoDisc, Inc.

Library of Congress Cataloging-in-Publication Data
Menconi, Al.
    Staying in tune : a sane response to your child's music / Alfred Douglass Menconi, David Steven Hart.
        p.   cm. — (How to win series)
    Previous ed. published under title: Today's music.
    ISBN 0-7847-0570-4
    1. Rock music—Moral and ethical aspects. 2. Contemporary Christian music. I. Hart, Dave. II. Menconi, Al. Today's music.
    III. Title. IV. Series.
    ML3534.M493   1996
    246'.7—dc20   96-7825
                                                CIP
                                                 MN

The Standard Publishing Company, Cincinnati, Ohio
A division of Standex International Corporation

03 02 01 00 99 98 97 96   5 4 3 2 1

Contents

Acknowledgements

I distinctly recall a day in the fall of 1977 when my wife handed me a pen, a spiral notebook, and said, "Okay, big talker, now you don't have an excuse not to write. Here's your pen and paper." That was nearly twenty years ago, and I'm still trying to record all my thoughts.

The first printing of this book was in 1990. It was entitled *Today's Music: A Window to Your Child's Soul.* Those who read it, enjoyed it immensely. We received scores of letters from families who used the teachings from this book as a means to develop better communication skills with their children. And that was its purpose: to help parents understand their children better and to communicate biblical values to them.

The problem was that very few people were aware of the book. Many saw it as a music book. Most bookstores listed it as such. Others saw it as an antirock book. The first printing never reached its potential because few people understood its true purpose. When the first printing sold out, the publisher chose not to reprint.

That's when God led us to Dale Reeves and Mark Taylor of Standard Publishing. They had read the book and thought that it fit perfectly in their "How to Win" series for helping parents communicate with their kids. These guys and many others at Standard have truly caught the vision for this book. What a blessing!

The new title, *Staying in Tune: A Sane Response to Your Child's Music,* communicates the true purpose of this book. Each chapter has been updated to reflect the changes that have taken place in the past six years.

In 1982, I started Al Menconi Ministries to educate parents, Christian leaders, and young people on the issues of rock music. I had no idea what I was getting into. Fortunately, God sent a couple of people my way to help in the work: Mike Atkinson, our first executive director and presently chairman of our Board of Trustees, and Dave Hart, research analyst supreme.

With Mike constantly challenging me to think through my opinions and Dave offering his own insights on secular music, I began putting my thoughts in print. Although I get most of the credit, there wouldn't be a book without the input of Dave Hart and Mike Atkinson.

I would write a chapter, Dave would rewrite it, and then Mike would edit and clarify it. The more I wrote, the more I realized that Dave was doing more than rearranging thoughts. He was adding valuable insights that he had developed in the years he spent researching and counseling at Al Menconi Ministries.

As you read this book, please understand that you are reading the research, insight, and experience of Al Menconi and Dave Hart. It is our prayer that this will be more than just another reading assignment. May it be a life-changing experience for you and your family.

♪   Thank you, Janice, for the love and support, as well as the pen and spiral notebook.

♪   Thank you, Ann and Allison, for the lessons you taught me about being a father.

♪   Thank you, Dale Reeves and Mark Taylor, for believing in me and in the value of republishing this book.

♪   Thank you to the Board of Trustees of Al Menconi Ministries for your love and direction.

♪   Thank you to the friends of Al Menconi Ministries for your prayers and support.

♪   Dave would like to thank his lovely wife, Velva, for all her love and support during this project.

♪   Finally, we would like to thank our Lord and Savior, Jesus Christ, without whom there wouldn't be a reason for life.

Introduction

Time does a lot of things to know-it-all, hotheaded men. Time has humbled this know-it-all to the point where I realize that God won't use a proud spirit. It has also changed the focus of my ministry and ultimately, the focus of this book.

In the early years of my ministry, I had a passionate antirock stance in regard to music. The things I wrote then reflected my attitude. Later, during the 1980s, I was basically pro Christian music, which became the focus of my writing. Now, after twenty-four years of ministry, I have finally realized that our main concern shouldn't be how *bad* the wrong kind of music is, or how *good* the right kind of music is. Rather, our concern should be how we can get our families to make the transition from wrong to right—in music and in every other area of life.

So this is not another book on rock music. Who needs another book to tell you how bad the music is that your kids are listening to? Instead, the goal of this book is to help you effectively communicate biblical values to your family using today's music as a window into their spiritual lives.

If you bought this book to gather information about all the nasty rock groups so you can manipulate your children into submission, you probably should return it. I don't think you'll find what you're looking for. But this book will show you how to better understand your child's spiritual needs by paying attention to the music he listens to. It will also provide insight as to how to deal with those needs. When that process happens, the music will take care of itself.

This book focuses on the necessity of the parent to communicate with the child. Dr. James Dobson regularly reminds us that typical parents spend less than five minutes a day in meaningful conversation with their children. It is my contention that most parents would gladly communicate with their children if they just knew how. This book will show you how.

You will learn how to develop a rapport with your children. You will discover how to speak their language. And you will find out how to encourage them to make wise, godly decisions that will promote spiritual growth. Please keep in mind that there is something worse than your children listening to rock music. It is far more serious to lose all communication with them and not be able to share the gospel of Christ.

This book does not offer instant solutions. In fact, the solutions offered will take time and hard work. Nobody said parenting would be easy, did they? But isn't your child worth the effort?

Al Menconi

Chapter 1

CONFESSIONS OF A FORMER RECORD BURNER

*"A number who had practiced sorcery brought
their scrolls together and burned them
publicly." (Acts 19:19)*

I mounted the chapel platform with eager anticipation. Seizing the podium, I surveyed the students seated anxiously in the auditorium. As a teacher and coach at this Christian school, I had a growing burden for the student body. Most of them already had a good idea what I would talk about in this chapel service. I was beginning to get a reputation on campus as a vehement antirock preacher. My compelling desire was to save my students from what had consumed my life until I was 26—godless rock music. I felt it had kept me from finding the joy of true salvation in Jesus Christ for so many years of my life, and I wasn't going to let the same thing happen to these young students.

It was obvious to me that many students in that room had already come to believe the myths of rock and roll promoting sex, drugs, and rebellion. I could see rock music's toll as I counseled students after school. The drama of broken family relationships and personal crises unfolded day after day. I knew that many parents were agonizing over their child's drift into immorality and rebellion. I was convinced that rock music was fanning the flames of sensual worldliness, leading students into involvement with sex, drugs, alcohol, and even the occult.

My text that morning was based on Acts 19:18, 19—the dramatic account of Christians in Ephesus who had torched their occult books in a bonfire as a public demonstration of commitment to their newfound Savior. I was convinced that believers in 1975 should be willing to make that same commitment by burning rock records. After all, wasn't rock music the twentieth-century version of the "black magic, incantations, and charms" *(TLB)* which had caused the Ephesian believers to stumble so long ago?

"If you're ever going to live for Jesus," I thundered at the students, "You must get rid of the music that binds you to sin! If you really love God, you'll destroy your rock music!"

As I pounded my point home, many of the students became visibly agitated. A few of them clearly thought I was some kind of nut. Others felt I was a righteous crusader for biblical truth and godly living. Some were disgusted. Some were motivated. Most were confused.

At the close of the message, I called for a schoolwide demonstration. "Tomorrow during lunch," I announced, "a trash can will be set up on the patio. I want you to pray about the matter, then bring any offensive records you need to burn."

The faculty members listened with a mixture of anxiety and dread. After chapel, the director of student activities tried to warn me of the consequences of this burn.

"Don't do this, Al," my friend advised. "We're going to have some real negative reactions to this."

"No, Ron," I responded with unswerving resolve, "I know I'm right and I'm willing to take the flak." I figured the negative response would be directed at me.

2

THE BURNING MOMENT

The following morning dawned sunless and gray. Classes came and went. Finally the burning moment arrived. Tension filled the campus as I rolled a dented metal trash can to the center of the school patio and waited. Gradually a curious crowd gathered, as if observing the scene of an accident.

A tenth-grade boy meekly stepped forward from the crowd of onlookers and dropped a Beatles album into my galvanized altar. Next came a timid girl with another album. As I watched the students, I began to pray that this would be a dramatic moment of decision. At last these students would be able to turn their hearts completely over to the Lord. Eventually twenty or thirty records and tapes had clattered to the bottom of the container. I began to realize that most were older albums, ones that would probably have been tossed out anyway. Masking my disappointment, I was determined to carry on.

I popped open the lid on a can of lighter fluid, sprayed the records with a dash of the combustible fuel, and lit a match. The sudden burst of angry flame surprised me, nearly catching my shirt sleeve on fire before I could jump back. But I stayed cool and waited for others to join in this celebration of "righteousness."

An eerie glow arose from the vinyl sacrifice and a foul smell accompanied the billowing black smoke. Remnants of Led Zeppelin, The Beatles, and The Who curled as the plastic melted. Those records would be silent forever; those students would be released from the barrage of lies which had washed over their minds day after day; families would be united; joy would replace frustration… or so I thought.

As I reflected on my triumph, I became aware of a rumble of discontent in the ranks of spectators. With dramatized agony, one student yelled, "Burn my Bible, don't burn Led Zeppelin!" Another called, "Let me buy those records, don't burn 'em." After twenty minutes and about forty melted records and tapes, one wise guy called the fire department. They didn't come, but the principal called a halt to the burn. I doused the fire, put the can back in its corner, and returned to class. But that wasn't the end—it was just the beginning.

WHAT WENT WRONG?

In the weeks following the record burning, I began to notice some unsettling results. I had hoped to enhance the faith of my students, but I had divided the school right down the middle. The students who had burned albums considered themselves quite holy. Others thought the record burners were fools. Among those who had participated in the record burning, the incident became a source of false pride. Those who burned several records saw themselves as being more spiritual than those who had burned only one: "I'm holier than you because I burned a Black Sabbath album and two Beatles records; you only burned one Led Zeppelin!" Those who burned one album saw themselves as better than those who didn't burn any records at all. It was all pretty ridiculous, yet sad as well. My idea had become a source of division instead of unity.

Most of the students' decisions to burn their albums were largely based on the emotion of the moment rather than a clear leading from the Lord. That fact became evident when most of those who had given up albums eventually restocked their record libraries with new albums.

Area newspapers gave the record-burning story front-page coverage. A photograph was later staged by a reporter with the *Los Angeles Times* showing me hammering a John Denver album to pieces. The story made the event resemble Hitler's book burning in Nazi Germany a generation earlier.

Some parents were alarmed by my tactics and phoned the school: "What's going on over there? Are you fanatics brainwashing our children?" Others threatened to withdraw their children.

What went wrong? I wanted to be a light to our world. Instead, people were viewing that light through the gray smoke of burning records. I had fed the press a sensational story, disgraced the school in the eyes of many in the community, and sown a negative attitude among the student body. Worst of all, I felt I had somehow disappointed my Lord.

Despite these unexpected setbacks, I was still sure I was right. The negative influence of rock music continued to crop up in counseling sessions with my students. Time after time I saw actions patterned after the immoral behavior of rock stars. Students showed allegiance by the vocabulary they used, the song titles printed on their book jackets, the posters they hung on their walls, the music they listened to in their cars, and the clothes they wore. They were hooked.

Teachers throughout the school could spot rock music's negative philosophies in student essays and creative writing assignments. Students would walk the corridors of school singing their favorite rock songs. At times it was as if the students spoke another language because of the buzzwords and key phrases that were known only to rock-and-roll insiders. By noting which group a student was "into," I could usually tell what type of problems he was experiencing—or could expect to experience. Rock stars (most of them moral degenerates) still had my students in their grip. And I still wanted to break the stranglehold.

Hadn't God said, "Shun profane and vain babblings: for they will increase unto more ungodliness" (2 Timothy

2:16, *KJV*)? What could be more worldly and empty than the records we had burned? What better way to "shun" ungodliness than to destroy the source of these evil messages? It seemed obvious to me that the music of The Beatles, The Rolling Stones, The Who, Led Zeppelin, Rod Stewart, and others were definitely "profane and vain babblings" because they advocated immoral sex, drugs, and rebellion.

Because of my public stand against rock music, I became a local celebrity at many churches in town. I was asked to speak to a number of church youth groups in the area. Many pastors, parents, and grandparents supported me for saying openly what they had been trying to say at home. But the young people simply grew defensive under my attacks. The more I spoke against rock music, the more they turned me off. They were repulsed by the aura of spiritual pride which had enveloped me— the kind of pride God hates (Proverbs 6:16-19). They were discouraged by my attacks, which were judgmental and condemning. Yet I fought on.

"How can you call yourselves Christians and still listen to this ungodly music?" I asked the young people in seminar after seminar. "Don't you understand what it's doing to you?" And they would simply shrug and respond, "Don't worry, it doesn't affect me. I just like the beat. I don't listen to the lyrics."

I wanted to force these young people to grow in the Lord, to develop a deeper relationship with Him, and to live a life that glorified Jesus Christ. That was my mission, but I was failing. With increasing fervor, I strained to convict my audiences about sin, righteousness, and judgment. For two years I struggled onward in my pilgrimage, with very little progress.

Immersing myself in the study of rock music, I accepted every invitation to speak. As the "expert," I became accusing, pleading, presuming, manipulating, and occasionally demanding. But it all came to a sudden halt one day when a girl approached me after a chapel session at my school. She told me, "It's not that we don't believe you, Mr. Menconi, but we just don't care."

That did it! I could handle criticism, but not apathy. If the Christian students didn't want to grow spiritually, why should I force them? If they didn't care, why should I? It was discouraging to always have kids think of me as a jerk. When I walked by their cars, they would turn their stereos up or down, depending on whether they mocked me or feared me. I was weary of having them talk about me behind my back, laughing at what I had to say.

Perhaps the record burning had not even been biblical. Had I only manipulated moods for the moment? What I thought was the fruit of my labors was turning sour. I had faced constant criticism. New record albums were going back on most of the students' shelves. It wasn't easy being called an idiot, a censor, and even a Nazi.

So I gave up. I quit accepting speaking engagements. I was tired of being a prophet no one listened to. I retreated to lick my wounds. It was hard enough to be a teacher, counselor, and coach without going out to speak on a complex subject that required so much research and preparation. I already had an excellent ministry working with the students in my classes and on the athletic field. My antirock crusade only seemed to be a distraction. Inside me arose a feeling of great relief when I decided to drop out. Like Jonah, I boarded a ship for "Tarshish" and sailed for less strenuous territory.

A SECOND CHANCE

A few months later, a good friend invited me to speak about rock music to his youth group at church. I turned him down. "I don't do that anymore, Jerry," I replied. "Kids today just don't care."

He looked surprised and then studied me carefully. He put his hands on his hips and asked, "Should the teens in my group listen to rock music?"

"No. I don't think so," I replied, "but I don't know how to get them to stop."

Jerry reached out and gripped my arm, "Well, Al, God didn't call you to be successful, just faithful. My kids need to hear your message." He continued, "I'm scheduling you to speak to my youth group in two weeks. You'd better get down on your knees and ask God to give you the right words. If they don't hear a message on rock music from you, who can I trust to tell 'em?"

Anyone but me, I thought. I wasn't looking forward to this assignment. But Jerry kept reminding me that Sunday was coming. ♩

Chapter 2

PROLOGUE TO A NEW STRATEGY

●

*"Don't let others spoil your faith and joy
with their philosophies, their wrong
and shallow answers built on men's
thoughts and ideas, instead of on
what Christ has said."*
(Colossians 2:8, TLB)

Boy, did I feel the pressure! Why did Jerry have to call me to speak to his youth group? Maybe God hadn't called me to be successful, but I was still tired of being a failure. I thought of all kinds of excuses to refuse Jerry's invitation. My convictions about the evil influences of rock music were as strong as ever, but my message had fallen upon deaf ears. I was scared of failing again.

I sat in my favorite chair with my Bible on my knees, praying and meditating about these things. My thoughts drifted to my loving Christian mother who for so many years tearfully pleaded with me to change my life. I lived at home in my late teens and early twenties, and would often come in at night drunk or loaded on drugs. As I staggered past my mother's bedroom, I would see her on her knees praying for me. Each time she would look up and ask, "Alfred, are you proud of yourself?" (My mother was the only person I allowed to call me Alfred.)

"Yeah, sure," I would answer with a drunken slur.

I thought of how my mother prayed for me every night of her life. It was amazing how faithful my parents were in their prayers. It was years after I moved away from home before those prayers were finally answered. Alzheimer's disease clouded my mother's mind before I made my commitment to Christ. I still wonder exactly how much she comprehended. She would tell those who visited her during those final days, "Alfred has become a missionary." Maybe she *did* understand. Nearly two decades later, it still pains me deeply when I remember how I hurt my mother all those years.

As I leaned back in the recliner, I recalled my care-free and irresponsible days in the mid-60s. I thought they would go on forever. I remember all the songs protesting the war in Vietnam, racial inequality, and other real or imagined wrongs. Strong feelings were expressed so beautifully in songs by Joan Baez; Bob Dylan; Peter, Paul, and Mary; and many others. I was right there tapping my foot to the beat, a college student searching for the endless party and making plans to change the world. "Sex, drugs, and rock 'n' roll" was more than a slogan to me. It was a way of life.

It wasn't that I didn't care about God. My parents were devoted Christians and I had attended church regularly, but I never really understood Christianity. At our church, emotions seemed to be the outward evidence of being truly spiritual. I "went forward" many times in search of a feeling that never came. I responded to invitations without knowing fully what "getting saved" meant or what the gospel of Jesus Christ was all about. Nobody really explained it to me. I finally concluded that I could never be saved because I no longer felt that little tug of the Spirit which my church taught me was necessary for salvation. Since I thought I was going to Hell anyway, I figured I might as well live like Hell.

After attending Pasadena City College in the late 60s, I selected San Diego State College for my upper division and graduate classes. I switched from a business emphasis to humanities and education classes so I could become more in tune with the social conscience of the 60s.

Drugs were plentiful at my new school. I cultivated a 60s look with long hair, a Fu Manchu mustache, and wire-rim glasses. I was labeled by my few remaining Christian friends as hopeless—beyond the reach of God's grace. I found out later that these "Christian friends" were actually praying that my girlfriend would dump me so they could witness to her better. To them, she looked like a Christian and I didn't.

I thank God that He didn't view me as my "friends" did. He saw beyond my problems to my need. As far as I know, my former girlfriend still doesn't know the Lord. I hope I never forget that it takes as big a miracle to save the clean-cut individual as it does to save the doped-out freak!

During this part of my life I stayed on campus as much as possible and found excuses not to visit Mom and Dad. But each Christmas I paid my respects by showing up during the holiday break. By 1971, Christmas vacation at home had become tedious. My father had nothing more to say to me and my mother was becoming progressively distant as Alzheimer's disease began to set in.

As soon as I could politely do so, I slipped away with some college friends. We had decided to go on a gambling fling to Las Vegas. I was eager to see how much I could win with $70. Happy to escape our mundane existence back home, we roared into Las Vegas counting our winnings before we even got out of the car.

But my excitement didn't last long. It quickly vanished with my cash at the blackjack table, along with the few dollars I was able to borrow from my friends. All too soon, my party was over. I watched TV in my hotel room for the rest of the weekend while my friends had fun downstairs in the casino. How boring! So much for my escape to good times. In my pursuit of happiness, all I found was emptiness.

To relieve my depression when I got back, I decided to clean my apartment and prepare for a new semester. As I was dumping trash into the bin out back, my neighbor asked me where I had been.

"Vegas," I mumbled.

"How'd you do?"

"Lost everything."

"Well," said my friend, "at least you had a good time."

Those words shattered my last delusion. No, I didn't have a good time. I had wanted the "good-time party" more than anything, but I had been lying to myself. Sex, drugs, and rock 'n' roll hadn't delivered the happiness I sought. I tried what the world said would make me happy, but I was miserable. I had avoided coming to Jesus Christ all those years because I was afraid it would end my fun, and where had it gotten me? Why not look at Christianity again? What did I have to lose?

HEAVEN CAME DOWN

Still terribly depressed, I went to my room and picked up the New Testament my mother had given me when I was a boy. I had never bothered to read it before, yet I treated it with respect. I never put my beer bottles on it, and I kept it dusted on the shelf. Now the time had come to see what it had to say.

I slumped into a chair with the Bible in my hands. Letting the pages flutter past, I prayed earnestly, "If there is a God, show me something." Honestly, that's what I did! In my simplemindedness, God took pity on me.

What happened next was not luck; it was His wonderful grace.

The pages stopped fluttering at Romans 10:9. I peered at the text for a moment, then read aloud: "That if you confess with your mouth, 'Jesus is Lord,' and believe in your heart that God raised him from the dead, you will be saved." Was that all? No crying? No funny feeling? No altar call? "Confess with your mouth, 'Jesus is Lord'... believe in your heart ... you will be saved." *If that's all it takes to become a Christian, I could have done that a long time ago!* I *did* believe in my heart that God had raised Jesus Christ from the dead. I wanted to make Jesus Lord of my life and be saved. So I did, and I was, and I am!

That night I slept peacefully for the first time in years. In the morning I awoke completely, totally, absolutely refreshed. Then I remembered the words of Romans 10:9 about confessing with your mouth. (I became afraid that the Lord might come that day before I had a chance to confess what I had done in my heart.) So I waited impatiently for my roommate to wake up. When he did, I let him have it.

"Hey, Tom, I became a Christian last night!" I exclaimed.

Tom stared with pity in his eyes. "I bet it doesn't last a month," he said. "You'll never give up your party lifestyle."

By faith I climbed farther out on a limb: "I'll prove it's real. I've decided to quit smoking, drinking, doing drugs, and listening to rock music."

I hadn't the slightest idea what Christianity demanded. All I remembered from my boyhood was a set of rules. You didn't do this and you didn't do that. But I didn't care at this point. I was willing to do or not to do whatever it was that Christ required.

In the next few weeks, Tom watched me closely to see if his prediction would come true. I was determined that it wouldn't, though I was still looking for the emotional experience that I had been taught to expect. I was so eager to please my Lord that I confessed my newfound faith in Jesus Christ to everyone I knew.

I dumped my booze, my cigarettes, and all of my secular record albums—The Doors, The Stones, Rod Stewart—the whole collection. I asked my parents to send me an old album by my uncles, the Palermo Brothers, who had been missionaries with *Youth for Christ* for many years. Their consistent testimonies and the godly life of my mother had reminded me that Christianity was truly real.

My father sent what I requested along with an album by Phil Kerr and the Harmony Chorus, one of my mother's favorites. I listened to those albums over and over again until the vinyl turned white. The music was quite a change from the rock and roll that I was used to, but I didn't care. It contained a message that was refreshing to my soul. I was absorbing truths of the gospel and was getting great results. Without realizing it, this music was encouraging me to grow in my relationship with Jesus Christ.

My commitment to Christianity lasted beyond the 30-day maximum limit that Tom had predicted. As I write this, it has lasted nearly 25 years and is going strong. My long search was over. I found the peace and joy I had been looking for by committing my life to Jesus Christ. As a bonus, I discovered the value of Christian music in helping me keep my mind focused on Jesus.

Later, a friend introduced me to the music of Andrae Crouch and the Disciples. The strong, biblical messages of his music were not only spiritually refreshing, but were also passionate and upbeat! I was beginning to realize that there was more to Christian music than church choirs, Phil Kerr, and the Palermo Brothers. Another friend introduced me to the Maranatha! Music albums and a group called Love Song. It was exciting to discover music that both ministered to me and was a joy to listen to. It was like having my cake and eating it, too!

Little by little, I filled my life with all types of Christian music. What a change from the rebellious sounds of the 60s! But the sound wasn't as important to me as the teaching that I eagerly sought. I wanted to follow Jesus Christ, and I enjoyed this music because it spoke to my heart, gave me joy, and taught me about living for Him.

In 1972 I finished my student teaching and discovered a Bible-believing church that was strong in the fundamentals of the faith. The fellowship with believers and the study of God's Word was like rain upon parched earth. I soon started to teach at the Christian school associated with the church.

BACK TO THE PRESENT

All these old memories made me realize why I held such strong views against the life I had left behind, including rock music. I genuinely regretted the sinful lifestyle of my past and I desperately wanted to save these young people from the same fate. That's why I had taken it upon myself to condemn secular rock and to warn against its excesses and evil influences. But somehow my message had become judgmental and rigid.

There in my recliner, I prayed for guidance. Later that night, as I was preparing for the upcoming message, I came across a verse: "Don't let others spoil your faith and joy with their philosophies, their wrong and shallow answers built on men's thoughts and ideas, instead of on what Christ has said" (Colossians 2:8, *TLB*).

Like a flash, the truth became clear. Isn't that what rock music is all about? What is rock music besides someone's thoughts or ideas set to a tune? And doesn't it usually offer wrong and shallow answers built on those thoughts and ideas, instead of on what Christ has said?

The Bible says that if these personal philosophies go against God's Word, they are empty. And if we constantly entertain ourselves with empty philosophies, they will eventually undermine our faith and joy in Jesus. As I sat there through the night and into the morning, I began to think about my presentation from the perspective of this important verse.

From this perspective, everything made more sense. The Bible didn't say that if you listen to Satanic music, you become a Satanist. The Bible didn't say if you listen to sexually perverted music, you become a sexual pervert. The Bible didn't say that if you listen to rebellious music, you become rebellious. The Bible says that if you choose to entertain yourself with philosophies that are against biblical values, you will struggle with your faith and your joy in Jesus Christ. As a Christian high-school counselor, I had to admit that struggling with their faith in Jesus and the joy of their salvation was the number one problem most of my students were experiencing. I don't know why I didn't see the connection earlier!

I had a week before I had to speak at Jerry's youth meeting. (He had not accepted my refusal and was still expecting me to come.) And now, with this new approach, I was looking forward to the challenge. My new message would not be about burning records and condemning audience members. Instead, I would encourage my listeners to examine for themselves the empty philosophies behind rock music and compare those ideas to God's Word.

Rather than condemning the music or my audience, I could have people evaluate for themselves. I would ask a variety of questions: "Does rock music influence you? How do you know, or do you ever stop to evaluate? How is your faith in Jesus Christ? How is the joy of your salvation? If neither your faith nor joy seems to be increasing, could rock music possibly be the reason? Does your choice of music go against biblical values?"

As a counselor and teacher, I knew the vast majority of students were struggling with spiritual questions: *How can I be sure I'm a Christian? Is there really a God? Will I really go to Heaven when I die? Have I lost my salvation?* Those who didn't struggle with faith were struggling with the joy of salvation. It was a rare student who exhibited the fruit of the Spirit—love, joy, peace, patience, kindness, goodness, faithfulness, gentleness, and self-control (Galatians 5:22, 23).

So with courage born of a new conviction, I was ready to tackle my next presentation. Jerry's youth group was normal (hostile, jaded, and well-churched), but I was pleasantly surprised by their response. Many of them made positive decisions about Jesus Christ and about their attitudes toward rock music! I didn't condemn or attempt to convict them. I left that to the Holy Spirit. I simply provided information about biblical principles for the Holy Spirit to use. Seeing lives being changed, I was ready to accept more speaking engagements with a renewed sense of mission and enthusiasm.

LETTING GOD BE GOD

The change of strategy in my seminars and counseling sessions was an exciting experience. Many who had struggled with their faith in Jesus began to listen to what I was saying and became committed to growing spiritually. I no longer felt compelled to manipulate my audiences into making emotional decisions. All I needed to do was contrast the empty philosophies of the musicians and their songs to the light of God's Word. Then the Holy

Spirit could show each listener how these philosophies were robbing him of faith and joy.

I now offer a simple prescription in all my seminars, just as a medical doctor would. I diagnose the problem (struggles with faith and joy), examine the symptoms (continual bombardment by empty philosophies), and offer a prescription (focusing on God's Word through Christian music). If the patient swallows the prescription, he is likely to get well (his faith and joy will be strengthened).

If you have a Christian family and/or responsibility for leading youth, or if you are a pastor or schoolteacher, you probably have the same questions I had: *Is all secular music evil? If so, what should I do about it? How do I know what is the right music to listen to? How do I keep my family away from evil music? How can I challenge young people to strengthen their faith and joy by listening to Christian music? Is all Christian music okay? What about Christian rock?*

The following chapters will answer these questions and more. You will find biblical insights and instructions, step by step, and you can examine God's Word on these issues. The Bible is true. God cares about you and your children. He will lead us to scriptural principles that are appropriate and effective for every situation. There is hope!

Chapter 3

THE
RUMOR
MILL

●

"Avoid foolish controversies." (Titus 3:9)

I had gone to conduct some music seminars at a Christian conference center. I hadn't gotten my luggage out of the trunk when a young man hurried toward me. I recognized him as a prominent youth pastor from Southern California. "Al! Al!" he called excitedly.

I closed the trunk and asked, "What's up?"

"You're just the man I need to see. Tell me, is there any truth to the story that a Satanic rock band had a revival service at the Los Angeles Forum and gave an altar call for people to dedicate their lives to Satan?"

This rumor was not new to me. I'd heard that some heavy-metal bands did that kind of thing at concerts as a sick joke. But at that point I had no documentation of public appeals for Satanism nor had it happened at any concerts that I'd seen. No one I trust has ever given me an eyewitness account of a Satanic altar call. I wasn't going to tell this young man something I couldn't document as fact. "I have no evidence that it happened," I said, "so if I were you, I wouldn't tell anyone that it took place. You don't want to communicate a half-truth."

"Well, if not in L.A., how about some other city?" he pressed.

"No, I still can't verify anything like that," I said.

A look of disappointment clouded his face for a moment, but then he brightened. With a shrug he said, "Oh, well, don't tell any of the kids here. I told that story last night at a meeting and a lot of them got saved!" Then he waved and was gone.

I've seen a lot of Christians use this tactic. Many preachers try to frighten people away from rock and roll by telling them gross or spooky stories—the scarier and more sordid, the better. It doesn't seem to matter to them whether the stories are actually true as long as they get across the point that rock music is really awful. The theory seems to be that if young people become convinced that rock music is really evil, they will automatically run from it and fall into the arms of Jesus.

But it doesn't usually work that way. Some young people who listen to rock music are already saved, or at least they think they are. They don't see rock music and Jesus as opposites! They believe they can embrace rock music *and* Jesus. Other youth are attracted by these weird, scary rock stories. Instead of being frightened away, they become even more curious about those groups and run right out to buy their records. Still other teens simply adjust their limits. They're glad to stick with the milder pop bands that only sing about sex and parties. None of that spooky devil music for them!

I had learned that the best way to get spiritual results is to show young people how desirable Jesus is. It is delightful to have Him forgive our sins and show us the way through our troubles! We discover great joy in living for the King of kings. Instead of focusing on how repulsive rock music is, we should demonstrate how valuable strong faith and joy in Christ can be. This way our children can make decisions about music based on positive goals rather than fear or deception.

As I carried my luggage to my cabin, I thought about that youth pastor. How sad that he was trying to make the ends justify the means! He didn't need to stretch the truth for the cause of Christ. It's just not necessary to say anything that can't be documented fully, no matter how tempting it is to motivate audiences by telling shocking stories. The truth is shocking enough.

Yet rumors continue to ricochet around Christian churches. They have so little evidence they would never stand up in a court of law. And Christians perpetuate them as though they were actual fact. Let's leave deception and fear in Satan's toolbox. We are called to imitate Christ by being faithful and honest in all things. We simply need to present the truth and let the Spirit do the rest.

IT'S ALL IN THE NAME

Some of the most popular rock music rumors are those that supposedly reveal the secrets of Satanism behind such groups as AC/DC and KISS. We still have people approach us at our seminars asking, "Is it true that AC/DC stands for 'Anti-Christ/Devil's Children'?" I tell them that the only place we've seen this information is in Christian books, but the authors never offer supporting evidence. What we've found in our research is not nearly so dramatic.

AC/DC was started by two brothers from Australia. Angus and Malcolm Young were two young, pimply-faced teens who wanted to make loud rock music for other young, pimply-faced teens. While trying to find a name for their band, one of the brothers noticed a tag on a vacuum cleaner (some sources say it was a sewing machine) that noted its AC/DC power. They wanted to be a powerful electric band and decided the initials described them perfectly (*People,* 1/30/84).

That's all there is to the story. It's not very spooky, is it? Based on this information, the best we could conclude is that perhaps AC/DC stands for Acne Can/Destroy Children! (But that's just a guess on our part!) Talk about straining gnats and swallowing camels! This band openly encourages rebellion and immoral sex, but some Christians want to hunt for secret signs of Satanism in order to prove that the band contradicts Jesus' teachings.

Another name that often crops up in the rock rumor mill is KISS. According to many antirock preachers, it means: "Kings (or "Knights" or "Kids") in Satan's Service." But that's simply not true. How do we know? Because Gene Simmons, the leader of the group, says it's not. To insist that Mr. Simmons is lying demands proof, and we have none. We must stick with the evidence we have, no matter how much we may dislike the group. No matter how tempting it is, we cannot simply make up stories in order to confirm our suspicions about them.

Besides, the truth about the origins of KISS gives us all the information (and ammunition) we need to evaluate them from a biblical standpoint. Back in 1971, the band was called Wicked Lester. After losing and replacing a couple of band members, the group decided to give themselves a new name. One day while traveling to a concert, one of them said, "Why don't we call ourselves the 'F-' word?" The others agreed enthusiastically. "Yeah, that would be great. That's what we got into rock and roll for—girls and sex!"

But one band member said, "Wait a minute. We can't call ourselves by that name. If we ever get an album contract, they wouldn't print that name on the cover. We're going to have to call ourselves the next best thing." So they came up with the name KISS instead (*Hard Rock Video*, 12/8/85). Remember that this was 1971. These days it seems that anything goes on an album cover.

KISS doesn't actually sing much about Satan or the occult. What they *do* sing about is sex, sex, and more sex. In fact, Gene Simmons claims to have collected over

2,000 Polaroid pictures of young girls (groupies) he's had sex with (*Newsweek*, 4/18/88). The facts about this group should be enough evidence for any inquisitive Christian. Why do some people feel it's necessary to make up Satanic stories to prove a point? After all, sin is sin. Scripture clearly reminds us, "The prudent sees the evil and hides himself, but the naive go on, and are punished for it" (Proverbs 22:3, *NASB*).

Another related rumor is that rock albums are often blessed by witches and become possessed by demons. Again, there is no credible proof for these accusations. The messages of many secular albums do not need a demon to be destructive to the believer. The empty philosophies and perversions should be more than enough to keep us away!

Too many Christians are missing the point. People can't adequately evaluate the sinful influences of today's music if they are only looking for blatant Satanism. Many parents are ignoring performers who present their perverted philosophies in more subtle packages. Many young people are becoming well-educated about occult signs and symbols, but they don't recognize sin when they see it. This preoccupation with the latest rumors, secret symbols, and gruesome details of Satanism tends to overshadow our focus on the beauty of Christ.

BACKWARD MASKING

Another persistent rock-and-roll rumor is the threat of backward masking. Some people insist that certain recordings contain one message when played forward, but quite another when played backward. Pursuing this argument is another waste of time.

In my seminars I play a portion of a song that is supposed to contain the clearest example of backward masking—"Stairway to Heaven," by Led Zeppelin. As the record plays forward, Robert Plant sings:

> Yes, there are two paths you can go by
> But in the long run
> There's still time to change the road you're on.

When this song is played backward, it is supposed to reveal a hidden Satanic message. I have recorded the song on reel-to-reel tape to play backward for the audiences at my seminars. First I play the tape forward while displaying the lyrics on a screen for all to see.

Next I play the message backward without suggesting any message. (In nearly all other rock music presentations where this is done, the speaker will say, "Now listen. You're going to hear 'My sweet Satan.'" Because of the power of suggestion, the listeners' minds are preconditioned to hear that specific phrase, and the audience invariably hears, "My sweet Satan.")

I don't provide verbal suggestions before I play this example of supposed backmasking. Then I ask if anyone heard a clear backward message. Very few people raise their hands. I ask if anyone heard something about Satan. A few more people will raise their hands. Finally, I ask: "How many people heard 'Abedy-goo-bop-surry-soup-eechee-dabbable-Satan'?" Everyone raises their hands.

Even when the song is played backward and slowed down, it is difficult to detect a message without being preconditioned to hear it. *So how is anyone going to hear it when the song is played forward at regular speed? Is a message really there? If so, how does it affect us? Does any scientific proof exist that we can be affected by backmasking? Is the concept of backmasked messages biblical?*

If a song contains a clear backmasked message, then everybody ought to hear it, right? And everyone ought to hear the same message. But the people who claim to hear this stuff don't all hear the same message. For instance, here are four different translations (from various published sources) of the same backmasked message of "Stairway to Heaven":

Version #1

Here's to my sweet Satan,
No other made a path
For it makes me sad,
Whose power is Satan.

(From Why Knock Rock? *Dan and Steve Peters with Cher Merrill, Bethany House Publishers.)*

Version #2

Here's to my sweet Satan,
There was a little child
Born naked and sad
Please now, I am Satan.

(From The Legacy of John Lennon, *David A. Noebel, Thomas Nelson Publishing Company.)*

Version #3

I sing because I live with Satan.
The Lord turns me off,
There's no escaping it.
Here's to my sweet Satan.
He'll give you six, six, six.
I live for Satan.

(From The Devil's Disciples, *Jeff Goodwin, Chick Publications.)*

Version #4

Oooh, Here's to my sweet Satan
The One whose little path
Has made me sad
Whose power is Satan
Oooh, my number, 666.

(From "The Occult in Rock Music" tape presentation, Eric Barger.)

25

In one of our seminars, a young man was convinced he heard something about shopping at Safeway! Preconditioned by his version of the message, we listened again. We're pretty sure we heard:

He's here to buy at Safeway.
Go on the lettuce aisle.
For Sears is bad.
See now, I am hatin' it.

It's all absurd, of course. Berke Breathed, cartoonist of the "Bloom County" comic strips, has poked fun at how Christians overreact to the backward-masking issue. (Can you blame him?) A character in one of his strips stated that he heard backmasking in a song which said:

Devil bunnies,
I snort the nose, Lucifer,
Banana, banana.

How foolish we appear to the non-Christian world. If a backmasked message is such a threat, then why are we hearing all of these different versions and having so much difficulty reaching an agreement? If we can't hear a clearly transmitted message, what's the point?

We can debate whether backmasking is real and/or harmful. I don't believe there is anything to be concerned about. Satan has kids singing about killing their mothers ("I Saw Your Mommy, and Your Mommy Was Dead," by Suicidal Tendencies, Frontier Records), raping their sisters ("Sister, Sister," by Prince, Warner Brothers Records), and worshiping Satan ("Spill the Blood," by Slayer, Geffen Records). These are just a few of the myriad of songs that, when played forward, contain destructive messages that ring loud and clear! Why care about backward messages in light of these other offenses? Some people, who insist there is scientific proof for it, confuse subliminal messages with backmasking. If you choose to believe in backward masking, that's fine. But this is a weak argument. And we're not going to win the war over rock music with weak arguments, no matter how much we believe them to be true.

THE BEST DEFENSE

It seems that as soon as you bring up the topic of rock music, you find yourself in a conflict. It might be an argument at home, a disagreement at church, or even a personal struggle. And no matter how mild or wild the tension might be, basically it's always a debate.

When I was involved in college debate classes, they taught me to line up my arguments in the order of their relative strengths. The strongest arguments went to the top, the weaker ones went to the bottom, and the weakest ones were thrown out.

Most rock-and-roll rumors are weak arguments. Accusations about "secret" band names, gremlins in the grooves, and backward masking are, at best, confusing and argumentative. We can go around and around on these issues and never come to a convincing conclusion. If we're going to deal with rock music successfully, we need to line up our strongest arguments.

Parents, your strongest argument is God's Word—not your opinion, not your taste, not rumors, not even the weird appearance of the performers. We simply need to examine the philosophies of the performers in light of God's Word. If those philosophies oppose biblical values, they will undermine the listener's faith and joy in Jesus Christ. Any other approach will only lead to an argument that can't be resolved.

So let's be careful. If we're going to say anything about someone's favorite performers or bands, we need to be certain that our arguments can be backed up by Scripture. I never argue about rock music. Never. When I rely on God's Word, there is nothing to argue about, nothing to debate. If somebody wants to disagree, they can argue with God rather than my opinion.

WISE COMMUNITY RESPONSES

On a flight to a seminar in Lincoln, Nebraska, I sat next to a lady from a southern city. When I took out my Bible, she told me she was also a Christian. She introduced herself and asked what I did.

I told her, "I speak to Christian parents about how to communicate with their children regarding the influence of rock music. In fact, I'll be in your city in a few weeks to conduct a seminar."

She opened her handbag and pulled out the front page of her local newspaper. It featured a story about Christian teens burning their records and videos— including one she really liked. Handing me the clipping, she asked, "Is this what you will be doing in our city?"

As memories of my record burning in San Diego paraded before me, I rushed to explain, "Oh, no! I don't believe in public demonstrations of that kind or in badgering people into conformity. Instead, I encourage them to make their own decisions. If a person feels led to destroy his or her own albums, that's fine." I pointed to the photograph in the newspaper and added, "I just don't think it should be done publicly."

"Why not?" she asked.

"Because no matter what reason is given for the burning, the public perceives it as the same type of demonstration that Hitler used when burning books in Germany. They suspect that you want to burn their records, too. And if people fear Christians, how are we going to reach them with the gospel?"

"I can understand that," my new friend said. Then she added wistfully, "But I can't understand why anyone would want to burn my favorite movie. I really enjoyed it and found nothing objectionable about it at all."

This Christian lady felt attacked because a movie she liked was being burned. It was as if she was wrong for enjoying it. I'm not sure that was the intent of the group who did the burning, but that's exactly how most people feel—attacked by those "record-burning" Christians.

Of course, as God convicts us about specific things, we must obey. If a person who attends my seminar feels the need to get rid of some offensive tapes, CDs, or videos, I certainly would encourage it. But the elimination of these influences should be done in private, not as an open show. By making a great public display out of these matters, we risk having others misunderstand. They look upon us as hypocrites because this kind of public display gives *us* the glory, not God.

Some people refer to Acts 19:17-19 and argue that public burnings are scriptural. They insist that Christians today should burn rock music in public just as the Ephesians burned their black magic and occult paraphernalia. (That used to be *my* argument.) But there is a difference between the scene in Ephesus long ago and the record-burning situations today. In Ephesus, Paul told people about Jesus, not the occult. The Holy Spirit convicted them about their practices. As a group, and without any prompting by Paul, they spontaneously decided to burn their evil books and idols.

Today we usually focus on condemning the occult. Then we cajole, sensationalize, and manipulate people into burning records. Instead of obeying the Holy Spirit, many people are only responding to the preacher.

The trouble is, the world just doesn't understand or care about our Christian concerns. They don't hold the same convictions. They don't understand even if the record burning is done in all sincerity. They only sense that someone's rights are being denied. Rock stars are seen as victims of an undeserved attack by "the church." And instead of creating genuine concern over rock music, we unintentionally create sympathy for "the poor rock star" who is being judged so unfairly.

It rarely does any good to go to the press, either. The secular media is not particularly interested in promoting Christian concerns. They love record-burning stories, but only because they sell papers. If you try to hold a press conference about your concerns, reporters will be all over you like a cheap shirt. They tend to encourage you to make emotional statements which some will twist to make it seem like Christians hate everybody. Many cast Christians as weirdos, prudes, and morally indignant fools who are out of touch with the times.

I don't want it said that I'm against getting rid of offensive music. But I do oppose doing so in public. We must remember we are called to glorify God and let sinners see Him through our lives by showing them our love. *How can a Christian show the love of Jesus to someone who feels he's being attacked?*

Our goal should be to encourage sinners to meet Christ, not to get them to conform to our values, likes, and dislikes. When we force our values on someone before he or she understands the heart of the gospel, we may create a roadblock that may never be broken down.

What, then, should Christians do? Do we roll over and let sin continue in the world uncontested? How can a Christian express displeasure concerning a profane rock performance without playing into the world's hands? These suggestions might be of some help:

1. ***Don't go to the secular press!*** Reporters are always in search of a sensational story, a controversy, an event.

2. ***Organize prayer groups to ask God to protect the community from the offensive***

group. Prayer gets results. We have heard of rock groups being rerouted and concerts being canceled or poorly attended because prayer groups met consistently to beseech God on behalf of the community. While you're at it, pray for the salvation of the rock stars. Remember, it took just as great a miracle to save *you* as it will to save *them.*

3. *Go to the people in charge of the concert facility and express your objection as a moral, concerned parent—but not as a Christian.* It's not that you are ashamed of Christ. But as a concerned moral individual, you can attract others who are also moral. All Christians may have strong morals, but all who have strong morals will not be Christians. Get other concerned parents to go with you. Having signed petitions in your hand will also help, especially if the promoters are appointed by elected officials.

4. *Educate your neighbors and parent/teacher groups.* Share your concerns with fellow church members, especially your youth leaders. Ask them to provide alternatives to rock concerts. Don't assume that Christian young people will avoid these concerts without some encouragement. Surveys of churches across the country have revealed that between 90 and 95 percent of Christian families contain at least one person who listens to secular music. Nearly 80 percent of that number listen to hard rock and dance music styles that include some of the most perverted and immoral artists today. Your education of other believers can make a big difference.

I hope you are beginning to see a difference in this approach to dealing with problems concerning rock music. Let me summarize briefly:

♪ Don't focus on sensational rumors. Simply tell people the truth in light of God's Word. We don't need to detail all the outrageous, horrible, bloodsucking aspects of rock music to convince people to reject it. Sensationalism may get an emotional reaction, but it rarely yields a genuine spiritual decision.

♪ Don't focus on the negative, which breeds fear, intimidation, anger, and hopelessness. Spend more time showing people the positive side of Jesus, creating a desire to draw closer to Him.

♪ Let the Holy Spirit do the convicting as others come face-to-face with Christ. When their lives change privately, quietly, and consistently, they become attractively different through the power of Jesus Christ. Their friends will then see the reality of those changes and inquire to find out what made the difference.

We can accomplish positive results if we honestly seek the truth. We must do our homework so we don't present confusing pictures. We need to avoid lumping everyone in the same categories or making generalizations that don't apply. All rockers are not Satanists. All sinners are not Satanists. All music is not Satanic. We are losing the battle with the rock generation because we don't always clarify our statements. With a commitment to truth, let's discover some facts about this music that has so much influence on our children. ♩

Chapter 4

THAT OLD BLACK MAGIC

●

*"Be self-controlled and alert. Your enemy the
devil prowls around like a roaring lion
looking for someone to devour." (1 Peter 5:8)*

A circle of robed figures chants and sways in the shadows. Their hoods hide the emotion in their faces, but there is evil in the air. In the center of the circle stands a sinister figure robed in red and black. Beneath him, a beautiful young woman struggles futilely against the chains that bind her to the cold stone altar.

The steel in the leader's eye and the arch of his brow only hint at the hideous power he holds. He mutters incantations in a language long lost in the mists of antiquity. He draws the cruel knife from its sheath and speaks as it shimmers in the cold candlelight. With one deft motion, he draws blood from the woman's arm and drains it into a silver chalice.

Mixing herbs and spells with the blood, he sips from the unholy cup. The chanting grows to a feverish pitch, drowning out the woman's helpless cries. Suddenly she freezes in catatonic terror. The sorcerer stands above her, the deadly dagger poised over her heart. With an exultant cry, he plunges the dagger downward and silences her screams forever.

At the mention of the word Satanic, the average American is likely to have this kind of melodramatic mental image. And yet perhaps the most common argument in the debate over today's music is that rock music is Satanic. This idea has been drummed into church minds for ten to twenty years now. It implies that most rock musicians are secretly Satanists.

To make this accusation is a weak argument. In the first place, the statement is so vague as to be almost meaningless. *What exactly is rock music? What does Satanic mean? How do we prove our accusation?*

Though many Christians use the terms Satanic and Satanist interchangeably, it is not entirely accurate to do so. The occult encompasses far more than the practice of Satanism. And biblically, the definition of Satanic is much broader than outright devil worship. Rock music today involves far more than spooky spiritualism.

At the root of the problem is the fact that our children usually know more about rock music and the occult than we do. Vague assertions and questionable claims are not going to convince them of anything. They need solid facts, real evidence, and biblical backing. We need to do our homework if we're going to provide real answers to legitimate concerns about rock music.

BACK TO BASICS—OCCULT 101

The word "occult" comes from the Latin *occultus*, meaning "things hidden, secret, and mysterious." It usually implies secret powers with religious implications from a realm that is hidden from ordinary living. The occult can include Satanism, witchcraft, Santeria, voodoo, the cabala, eastern mysticism, mystery religions, New Age meditations, and, depending on a person's perspective, some forms of parapsychology.

People usually become involved in the occult through curiosity or by deliberately seeking the special powers they believe can be found in the prescribed ceremonies. The powers are believed to offer something that is out of the ordinary, something hidden from others.

The darker side of the occult is probably best represented by Aleister Crowley (1875–1947), a magician who considered himself the most wicked man on earth. Crowley attempted to practice every type of magic known to man. If anyone ever sacrificed babies to obtain demonic power, it was Crowley. He called himself the Beast and considered himself to be the most powerful master of the dark forces who ever lived. But to his contemporaries, he was an insufferable braggart and a second-rate magician. He was booted out of numerous organizations and countries. He died in poverty and obscurity in his home on the shore of Loch Ness, Scotland.

He has achieved recognition over the last couple of decades through certain rock artists. The Beatles featured him on the cover of their *Sergeant Pepper's Lonely Hearts Club Band* album. Ozzy Osbourne sang praises to "Mr. Crowley" on his *Blizzard of Oz* album. Led Zeppelin guitarist Jimmy Page moved into Crowley's house after it was abandoned for 20 years because it was believed to be haunted and cursed. Page also owns some of Crowley's robes, books of spells, and other occult paraphernalia (*Hammer of the Gods,* Stephen Davis, Ballantine). Sting, formerly with the band The Police, is also reported to have quite a fascination with Crowley.

Another admirer of Crowley is a man named Anton La Vey, a former lion tamer and carnival organist who authored the *Satanic Bible.* He also founded The Church of Satan on April 30, 1966. This San Francisco-based church gave rise to a number of organized groups open to the public for the ceremonial practice of Satanism. These churches are perfectly legal and tax-deductible. They also promote themselves as the only type of Satanism actually being practiced in America today, which is simply not true. Satanism is practiced on at least four different levels:

1. *The organized church of Satan and its variants.* These groups, such as The Church of Set, are registered, open to the public, often monitored by authorities, and sometimes listed in the *Yellow Pages*. They vehemently deny the existence of any form of organized, underground Satanic activity.

2. *Underground Satanism.* This level of Satanism comes in two varieties: generational and professional. Underground Satanists are highly secretive and organized covens composed of a variety of local seekers including blue-collar workers, housewives, and even professionals like doctors, lawyers, CPAs, police officers, and elected officials. Included among these underground Satanists may be a certain number of generational Satanists from specific family groups, with practices passed on from generation to generation and priestly responsibilities passed from father to son.

   Both generational and professional Satanists may also participate in illegal operations such as drugs, prostitution, and pornography. These groups are suspected of all sorts of heinous crimes, including human sacrifice. Details on these crimes are sketchy and difficult to substantiate, but a growing number of defectors and surviving victims are providing evidence for their existence and their illegal schemes.

3. *Self-styled psychos.* Perhaps the most publicized and best-documented Satanists are people like Charles Manson and Richard Ramirez (the Night Stalker). They tend to create their own brand of hodgepodge occultism to justify their need to act out psychotic fantasies. Proponents of Satanic churches tend to write off these types as insane exceptions. They warn us not to generalize from such rare cases, but they don't seem to notice that the "rare exceptions" are popping up more frequently.

4. *Teenage dabblers.* Some Satanic activity comes from teens who operate alone or in small groups, practicing spells, raiding graveyards, leaving a spray-paint trail of Satanic graffiti, and occasionally engaging in animal mutilations. Teen dabblers are spurred on by horror movies and some types of hard-rock music, and are almost always under the influence of drugs and alcohol.

As one police officer put it, "Lots of teens listen to heavy metal and never get into the occult. But I've never caught a teen involved in occult-related crimes who wasn't also involved with heavy metal." Music that focuses on bizarre forms of the occult and Satanism often produces a curiosity that hooks some teens into a deeper search for mystical powers.

While Satanism gets a good deal of publicity, it is by no means the only form of occultism practiced in America today. The occult includes a variety of forms, philosophies, and theologies. Witches believe completely different things than Satanists about God and the universe. Some occultists are into forms of Hindu beliefs, Buddhist beliefs, and other types of eastern mysticism. Deuteronomy 18:10, 11 forbids all these practices. It would be fair to say that these practices are "Satanic," since Christian theology ascribes all such practices to the devil as their source and inspiration. It is not accurate, however, to say that all occultists are Satanists.

Each occult practice has its own flavor of philosophy, goals, and rituals. To indicate that they are all the same would show our ignorance, especially to those (including our own teens) who have studied such things. It would be like telling a chef you can't tell one spice from another, so it really doesn't matter what he cooks with. We must be more perceptive if we're going to persuade our kids to honestly evaluate their favorite rock stars.

THE ROARING LION

It is a weak argument to call people Satanists simply because we don't understand the philosophy they promote. It weakens the argument even further to insist on an emotional opinion in lieu of documentation. A preoccupation with Satanism in rock may even make you a tool of Satan's devices, though that's the farthest thing from your intentions. In the struggle over rock music, many Christian parents are becoming victims of Satan's roaring-lion techniques. Let me explain what I mean.

Lions hunt in groups called prides, and for some reason they are paranoid of being surrounded. They won't jump into the middle of a helpless flock of sheep or goats because it drives them crazy to be surrounded on all sides, even by frightened animals. They prefer to get an animal away from the flock, then they attack.

A frequent tactic is to get an old toothless lion on one side of the flock, usually up on a rock or in another visible spot, and have him roar his head off. Meanwhile the younger lions are hiding in the high grass on the other side of the field where the unsuspecting flock is grazing. Any animal foolish enough to bolt away from the flock seeking shelter from the toothless roar will be caught and killed by the more dangerous lions.

Satan doesn't mind doing a little roaring. Sometimes he'll make himself as obvious as possible. This causes some people to run off in a wild riot of terror. Others are irresistibly drawn to the power the lion displays. Still others have learned that the lion is always toothless, and they arrogantly conclude that there is nothing to fear from lions (never realizing the lions who have blended into their surroundings are far more dangerous than the one in plain sight).

Satanic influences in rock music have become a roaring lion in many Christian circles. We have become so focused on occult symbols and blatant Satanism in hard rock that we often miss the other dangerous "lions" which lie in the grass of more widely accepted forms of entertainment: sexual immorality, depression, suicide, rebellion, materialism, apathy, hopelessness, and carelessness, to name a few.

Hasty conclusions about Satanism based on images from fairy tales and horror movies can also become a roaring lion. Too great a focus on the human-sacrificing elements of classical Satanism may only cause us to miss other (more subtle) forms of the occult. Many philosophies present a potential danger to the faith of evangelical Christians. Our children are continually exposed to such philosophies and may be eagerly exploring them. We cannot ignore these lions in the high grass, just because Satanism is the most obvious extreme.

Of course, if the occult is a problem in a Christian home, it must be dealt with. There are many good books and organizations that can help. But keep in mind that rock music is not always an occult issue. All rock stars are not Satanists. Satan can entice us to do evil in ways other than ritualistic Satanism. And there are better ways to deal with the problems of rock music than simply accusing every secular artist of being a Satanist.

MODERN-DAY WITCHCRAFT

There was a time when educated, middle-class Americans simply did not believe in ghosts, the devil, or the occult. It was considered too superstitious for modern thought. A large segment of the population still considers these beliefs silly or superstitious, and would never consider indulging in bizarre activities connected to this unseen world. Ironically enough, many young people who wouldn't be caught dead at a séance are practicing forms of modern-day witchcraft without even knowing it. Let's consider the widespread teenage practices of sexual activity, drug use, and rebellion.

Sex and the Satanic Sacrifice

Many teens and young adults consider sexual freedom and the party lifestyle "normal." They may not know it, but they are ascribing to the philosophy of hedonism—"eat, drink, and be merry, for tomorrow we may die." They are motivated to practice the hedonistic lifestyle for different reasons: peer pressure, hyperactive hormones, the need for acceptance, or the desire to be different. Many make some foolish and heartbreaking decisions. But they don't usually realize that they may also be practicing a modern-day form of witchcraft.

Sexual activity is central to the hedonistic lifestyle. Young girls are experiencing pressure to have sex at earlier ages. Teenage pregnancy and sexually transmitted diseases continue to occur at epidemic proportions

despite (or perhaps because of) all the sex educ
available in the schools. The assumption is that being a
virgin is not cool and that sexual intercourse makes a
young person an adult. With alarming ease, this message
draws teens into the practice of something very much
like the occultic virgin sacrifice.

The virgin sacrifice is central to many ancient
occult practices. The occultist bent on controlling the
dark forces desires the corruption of innocence. With
the exception of hurting innocent babies, there is no
better way to destroy purity than by the violation of a
virgin.

In the occult ceremony, a pentagram is drawn on the
floor around an altar, or perhaps on the stomach of the
victim. The pentagram becomes the focal point from
which the "power" or demon will be drawn. A circle is
drawn around the five-pointed star to ensure control of
the demon once it arrives.

After ceremonious chanting, candle burning, and
symbolic bloodletting, the "virgin" is sexually assaulted
by all the members of the coven. The victim is sometimes
a volunteer from the coven, but an unwilling victim constitutes a greater sacrifice and therefore yields greater
power. The victim is often drugged, beaten, and psycho-
logically manipulated to make her manageable.

And the victim is not always a young lady. Homo-
sexual covens exist as well. While these actions may
seem too horrible to be believed, more victims are beginning to surface and testify to the reality of these practices
in America today.

Of course, the average party-minded teen isn't interested in serving Satan in this or any other way, yet the
results remain the same. Virginity is sacrificed in one
way or another, and Satan doesn't care if it happens on a
cold stone altar or in the backseat of a hot Chevy. The
destruction of innocence is accomplished.

Do you see why we should be as concerned with music that promotes immoral sex as we are with music that promotes Satanic ritual? In God's eyes, they're the same kind of sin.

The Drug Connection

The drug problem in our country is so severe the government spends billions of dollars to deal with it. Recreational use of drugs and alcohol (and alcohol is a drug) is especially extensive among teenagers today, and such regular use rarely remains casual. Teens are overdosing at an alarming rate, and parents are spending millions on rehabilitation for their teens. The tragedy of drug abuse can also find a parallel in the world of witchcraft.

In the Greek version of the Old Testament, the word for witchcraft is *pharmacea,* from which we get the English word *pharmacy*. Even 4,000 to 6,000 years ago, the link between drugs and witchcraft was clearly recognized. Some early uses of drugs by witch doctors and shamans evolved into legitimate medical treatments. But ancient forms of witchcraft used drugs to control the demons responsible for illness.

Sometimes drugs were administered to patients in the belief that they would strengthen them to wrestle with the spirits causing the sickness. Drugs were taken by witch doctors to put them in contact with the spirit world—to combat the demons in their own domain. In either case, the drugs were intended to lower the human spirit's ability to resist the spirit realm.

Aside from the physical dangers of drug use, drugs can also create a condition that makes people more vulnerable to demonic realms. Even in the earliest stages, drug use creates a condition that keeps the user dependent on something besides God. In the worst cases, drug use can open a person to oppression by demonic forces.

Modern-day practitioners of the occult still use mind-altering drugs to induce an altered state of consciousness to make them more receptive to the spirit realm.

Most teens do not take drugs to meet demons. If anything, they would like to escape the feeling that there are too many demons in their lives already—demons of inadequacy, fear, depression, rejection, responsibility, parents, and grades. Unfortunately, their heartaches only grow worse with continued drug use.

Whether the user is consciously practicing witchcraft is irrelevant in light of the results. The facts are that teens are becoming dependent on drugs instead of God. Their resistance to evil is lowered. They are being exposed to the demonic realms. And innocence continues to be violated.

Rebellion

Even before Marlon Brando became a "wild one" or James Dean raced to his fate as a rebel without a cause, teens and rebellion have been seen as synonymous. It's as if the culture is saying that teens are supposed to be rebellious and music has to fuel the fires of that rebellion. Today's entertainment media, peer pressure, and even the focus of education in today's schools certainly make it difficult for teens to make a smooth transition from childhood to adulthood.

Youthful passions, combined with the normal frustrations of life, can leave teens restless and anxious. Today's teens live in an insecure time, as evidenced by the growing divorce rate and fracturing of families, the homeless problem, teen pregnancy, AIDS, global warming, depletion of the rain forests, and the increasing death rate due to drugs and suicide. The sense that our society is quickly getting out of control can make anger and defiance seem like the only natural responses. Teens want answers, and they want them now.

Rebellion offers a quick and easy solution—a sense of power and the illusion of being in control. The power of intimidating an adult provides freedom from the pressures that suffocate the average young person, but there is always a price to pay for this kind of freedom. The "endless" party always ends and the piper always gets paid.

Rebellion is not exclusive to teenagers. It is present every time anyone resists the call of wisdom (Proverbs 1:20-33). God calls us to conform to the character of His Son, yet we preoccupy ourselves with a search for shortcuts. In His sight (and in His Word) that rebellion of heart is the same as the heart of witchcraft (1 Samuel 15:23). Why? Because whether we are caught up in the ceremonies of witchcraft or the machine of materialism, rebellion results in the sin of selfishness.

Reliance on self always separates us from God. Satanic influence goes far deeper than the secret ceremonies of Satanism. They are rooted in selfishness. Let's consider the meaning of "Satanic" from one more angle.

"DO WHAT THOU WILT"

A Christian police officer in San Diego, assigned to investigate occult crimes in the county, gave a fellow officer a copy of Anton La Vey's *Satanic Bible*. After reading it, the officer (who was not a Christian) was puzzled. He said, "I don't see what all the fuss is over this book. It made a lot of sense to me."

The policeman's reaction is not a rare one. The book does not live up to the hideous terror of Satanism that we have concocted in our imaginations. Anton La Vey was not trying to write a spooky book. It is so practical and philosophical, it bores many teens who pick it up expecting a mystical fairy book. La Vey was trying to express what he felt was the reasonable side of Satanism. He sees it as a practical philosophy for taking care of yourself in an uncertain world. It blends in with the world around us so well that many adults do not recognize the real danger hidden in the pages.

According to La Vey, the key to a Satanic way of life is found in the "Nine Satanic Statements" (a mockery of the Ten Commandments). Since the first commandment of the *Holy Bible* is to worship no one but God, we might expect the first Satanic statement to command worship to no one but Satan. But this is not the case.

The first statement reads: "Satan represents indulgence, instead of abstinence." This is an echo of Aleister Crowley's infamous proclamation in *The Book of the Law:* "'Do what thou wilt' shall be the whole of the law." And it sounds amazingly similar to the credo of American commercialism—"have it your way."

This philosophy stands in direct contrast to the Bible. Jesus says, "If anyone would come after me, he must deny himself and take up his cross and follow me" (Matthew 16:24). If we are going to obey Colossians 2:8, we must learn which philosophies can spoil our faith and joy by comparing them to the message of Jesus' teachings. Jesus says deny yourself. La Vey says indulge yourself. The *Holy Bible* teaches us to control our lusts. The *Satanic Bible* says to pursue our lusts. The Word of God says to feed your spirit. The world says to feed your flesh.

Here we arrive at the key to understanding what is actually Satanic. Let us no longer limit ourselves to a pre-occupation with occult symbols and extreme portraits of evil rituals. Whether it comes from Satanism, witchcraft, rock and roll, or a TV commercial, any philosophy that teaches us to place self above God is Satanic.

Selfish pride is part of Satan's nature. It led to his downfall and then to the fall of Adam and Eve. A self-serving attitude is incompatible with a servant's heart. To "do what thou wilt" is outside the will of God.

We can help our children understand this important contrast by setting up the image of a teeter-totter. Colossians 2:8 is the central fulcrum on which we rest our faith. As we encounter various ideas and philosophies, we put them on the plank that rests on the fulcrum. Depending on how each philosophy matches up to what Jesus teaches, it will either teeter or totter.

At one end of the teeter-totter lies the philosophy of the *Satanic Bible*—live for self, die to Jesus. On the other side of the teeter-totter lies the philosophy of the *Holy Bible*—die to self, live for Jesus.

Now we can examine the philosophies of our favorite artists. What is the basic philosophy of Janet Jackson, Mariah Carey, Boyz II Men, Snoop Doggy Dogg, Green Day, Nine Inch Nails, the Cranberries, or Hootie and the Blowfish? Examine the message of each artist. Is it closer to the teachings of the *Satanic Bible* or the *Holy Bible*? Does it teeter or totter?

As we take this approach, we can skip the arguments that call on us to prove whether an artist is a bona fide Satanist. These arguments always erupt into World War III anyway. They don't strengthen our faith or our families. But the teeter-totter is an easy way to measure the spiritual impact of groups, even if the groups have absolutely nothing to do with rumors about the occult.

Do your teen's favorite groups teeter or totter? How about your favorite groups, parent? Are your family's favorite entertainers actually closer to the philosophy of selfishness? If that's the case, the *Holy Bible* says that if you continue to entertain yourself with such philosophies, it will eventually undermine your faith in Jesus Christ and the joy of your salvation.

This is an essential concept to understand when we deal with our children about rock music. We don't have to present the extreme edge of evil in every song to prove our case. (They've already heard those arguments and know which ones aren't true.) What is true is that much of what the world teaches can destroy our faith and joy. Such worldly philosophies do not have to be as ominous as the occult or as immoral as adultery. They can be as simple as selfishness. And such teachings do not lie in the realm of hard rock alone. The seeds of selfishness are planted in every musical field. In fact, they are all around us in every aspect of the world (even the church).

THE MISSING GOSPEL

We should not expect to find evil around every corner, or Satan under every rock. Don't allow the roaring lion to distract you as he does so many others. A preoccupation with exposing evil can keep us from giving our kids what they really need. We need to teach them the difference between wrong and right. But just because we show them what to run from, doesn't mean they know what to run toward. They need a clear picture of who Jesus is, what He did, and what life with Him can be like.

Our kids need a more complete gospel, a more fulfilling hope. Too often we indicate that the church is for people who don't do bad things anymore. This can be a grave mistake. It leaves young people with the impression that real Christians are people who "don't smoke or drink or chew, or go with girls who do!"

But the cemeteries are full of those who can make the same claim! If our churches are only concerned with the avoidance of evil, no wonder so many young people see them as dead. Christianity is far more than a list of bad things we don't do anymore.

Yes, it's true that Jesus saves us from the fires of Hell. He saves us from the penalty of sin. He saves us from the dire consequences of our own foolish choices, time after time. But there's more to our salvation than a focus on what we were saved from.

Just what are we saved to? Didn't He come so that we might have life and have it more abundantly (John 10:10)? Weren't we set free so that we could live dynamic, exciting lives for Christ while we remain in the world? Aren't we also looking forward to spending eternity with the One who loves us more than life itself? Aren't we to live so we might give Him glory?

If we are too preoccupied with the search for sin, what does that say about the focus of our faith? If we live in a perpetual state of criticism and fear, what are we telling our children about our hope? If we drag ourselves through the dull duties of Christian obedience, what are we revealing about our joy? If we measure our Christian testimony only by the things we give up for God, where is the fruit of our salvation today?

We cannot call everything Satanic and expect our children to automatically run to Jesus. We must offer real hope, alternatives, and answers. We cannot assume that they understand the eternal consequences of their choices just because we go to church and try to live good lives. We must show them Jesus. They must see our faith and joy as part of an abundant life with a living Lord.

If we are going to deal with rock music in our homes, we need to do our homework about the role of rock music in our lives. We need a sense of history. We need to know what today's groups are really saying.

Ultimately, this battle is not about sex and Satanism, personal tastes in music, or who's right and who's wrong. It is about the eternal future of our children. We are not trying to save young people from rock and roll. We are trying to lead them to our beloved Savior.

Chapter 5

A BEGINNER'S COURSE IN ROCK AND ROLL

*"For the time will come when men
will … gather around them a great number
of teachers to say what their itching ears
want to hear." (2 Timothy 4:3)*

Selfishness and immorality are far more consistent with Satan's strategies than drinking blood or drawing pentagrams. Musicians don't need to be practicing Satanists to conflict with the teachings of Jesus. Yet by doing a little homework, any mature Christian can still evaluate today's music in the light of God's Word. A realistic sense of music history and an understanding of the times will provide an accurate picture of what the world has been teaching our children through music.

Rock music is actually rooted in the rhythms of the black church. For two centuries, black slaves expressed their heavyhearted desire for freedom in work songs and church spirituals. These intensely moody melodies gave rise to the blues and many later forms of soul music.

In contrast to this music, there was also the energetic and passionate release expressed in the frantic call and response of the "ring shout." Shuffling feet and shaking bodies became an integral part of a fervent church experience that came to be known as gospel music. In the 1930s and 1940s, many black musicians began to perform publicly in roadhouses and nightclubs. Those who had been raised in the churches began combining the familiar energy, passion, and rhythms of gospel music with more worldly lyrics and lifestyles—a combination that gradually evolved into jazz, boogie-woogie, rhythm and blues (R&B), and eventually rock and roll.

It is generally accepted that the term "rock and roll" began as a euphemism for sexual intercourse. ("Jazz" was a Cajun word for the same thing.) Yet much evidence suggests that even this secular phrase had its roots in the church.

In their book, *Stairway to Heaven* (Ballantine), Davin Seay and Mary Neely refer to a 1934 version of a gospel tune called "Run, Old Jeremiah" with the lyrics: "Oh, my Lord! Oh, my Lordy! Well, well, well! I've gotta rock! You've gotta rock!" And back in 1922, a blues-styled number by Trixie Smith was called "My Daddy Rocks Me (With One Steady Roll)" and a gospel song by Clara Smith was titled, "Rock, Church, Rock."

The various opinions expressed by musicians, musicologists, sociologists, psychologists, and religious figures indicate that we still don't have a very good definition of exactly what constitutes rock-and-roll music. Musicologists give some general guidelines to define the style in terms of rhythm and structure, but they leave us with the idea that it is something you must have a "feel" for. Most Christians who write about rock music rarely try to define it in musical terms, leaving us with the idea that rock music is whatever they don't happen to like.

It is also difficult to pinpoint the first real rock-and-roll song. Ike Turner (former spouse of Tina Turner) claims that his 1951 tune "Rocket 88" was the original. Author Davin Seay points to the New Orleans sounds and a blues-bred shouter named Roy Brown who wrote and recorded "Good Rockin' Tonight" back in 1947. Some people suggest that the credit goes to Big Joe Turner, who took boogie-woogie jump-blues into the mainstream music market in the late 1930s and recorded such hits as "Shake, Rattle, and Roll" in the early 1950s. Others give credit to early blues artists like Robert Johnson, Leadbelly, Muddy Waters, Howling Wolf and Blind Lemon Jefferson.

But for the white, middle-class audience, rock and roll probably first reared its raucous head in a movie about high-school hoodlums called *Blackboard Jungle*. The film featured a rockabilly tune called "Rock Around the Clock," by Bill Haley and his Comets. Haley had started out with country swing bands, but after recording Ike Turner's "Rocket 88" and Big Joe Turner's "Shake, Rattle, and Roll," he became convinced "that high-energy music which kids could sing along to, clap to, and dance to— something like black R&B—would prove popular" (*The Rolling Stone Encyclopedia of Rock & Roll*, edited by Jon Pareles and Patricia Romanowski, Rolling Stone Press/Summit Books).

Haley proved to be right, but he didn't profit from his prediction. His American career lasted only about three years after his #1 hit in 1955. He just wasn't the typical teen idol. He was overweight, balding, and had already turned 30 before he really got started in rock and roll. Even though his success in Britain and during oldies revival tours resulted in sales of sixty million records, he died in 1981, a broken man. But *Blackboard Jungle* and the song "Rock Around the Clock" had already begun to link the ideas of rock music and teenage rebellion in the minds of many concerned parents. Rock music became the kind of thing "those kinds of kids" listened to.

The 1950s and early 1960s saw a continuing pattern of black church music turning to black secular music turning to teen rock music. A host of black artists raised in the church began to record R&B and pop tunes.

Musicians like Little Richard, Sam Cooke, Chuck Berry, Ray Charles, James Brown, and Aretha Franklin all learned their unique styles singing in the church.

Sam Phillips, a record studio owner, noticed this trend long before most record producers. He realized that he could reach a large young white audience if he could just find a white man who could sing with the passion of a black singer. And he found one—Elvis Presley.

The young truck driver recorded a demo for his mother in Phillips's studio in 1954 and rock history was made. His rockabilly influences made the music more palatable to white teens, especially in the South. But it was his Pentecostal fervor that really grabbed their attention. Elvis's famous pelvis gyrated as a symbol of the pent-up passions and romantic ideals of his energetic young fans.

If Elvis was the one who freed rock and roll from Pandora's box, Jerry Lee Lewis was responsible for seeing that it spread. His no-holds-barred style of performing set the pace for rock-and-roll excess in the years to come. It is important to remember that both Elvis and Jerry Lee were raised in Pentecostal churches. The rock-and-roll fire they were fueling was first fed by the religious fervor of their churches.

Many parents became shocked and even outraged by the frantic energy and worldly excess of this music. An especially strong outcry came from the church because of the immorality implied by these songs and the lifestyles of the artists who performed them. However, in those days, the church did not usually argue that rock was the devil's music. The popularization of mysticism and the occult was yet to come in America. "Sex, Drugs, and Rock 'n' Roll" was not yet an anthem for young people, nor had electric amplification become widespread.

Parental concern at this point was for the frantic pace of the music and the way the young people responded to it. Soon the objection of "the beat" became universal. But the concern was not that the music had a demon beat, but rather that it contained a jungle beat.

What should have been legitimate concern over morals and rebellion became a racial issue. In those days, there was pop music and there was "race" music. When DJs like Alan Freed tried to introduce white teens to black "race" music, he faced intense objections from parents. Some saw "race music" as the heritage of those primitive, wild-eyed savages who were only one step away from the jungles of Africa.

R&B did little to ease a parent's mind because black artists tended to be more blatant about sexual affairs in their lyrics. Many black jazz musicians were using drugs and alcohol long before rock music came along. Their morals were not any looser than their white counterparts, they just had the audacity to sing about it openly.

The classic example is Hank Ballard's "Work with Me, Annie." The lyrics were a blatant request for sexual favors. And if anyone had questions about what kind of work Annie was being asked to do, Hank's next single removed all doubt: "Annie Had a Baby and She Can't Work No More."

In response to parental concern over race music, the music industry decided to "sanitize" the music by cleaning up the lyrics and providing positive, clean-cut role models to sing them. For instance, the Hank Ballard song was changed to "Dance with Me, Henry," a 1955 hit for Georgia Gibbs (and an early example of the rock-and-roll trend of using "dancing" as a euphemism for having sex).

White groups began to rerecord more "race music" hits to make them accessible to white teens. For instance, "Earth Angel," by the Penguins (a Los Angeles R&B group) was recorded by the Crew Cuts (a white Canadian group). "Silhouette," originally sung by the Rays (a New

York R&B group), was redone by the Diamonds (another white Canadian group). Even Pat Boone had a couple of clean hits from Little Richard's raunchier versions of "Tutti Frutti" and "Long Tall Sally." There are dozens of other examples.

The practice of white artists recording songs originally done by black artists became known as "covering" a song. The moral leaders of the day weren't as offended by the clean-cut white artists as they were about the original black singers. The simple fact is that they didn't want their children to idolize a "Negro." Yet many young people of that day will confess to having Pat Boone's records out on their nightstands, while they kept Little Richard's versions in the bureau drawer under their socks!

Rock music gained its identity in the mid-1950s and began to be associated strictly as teen music. Though nobody particularly saw it as devil music, there was a definite trend toward rebellion and sexuality that should have gotten the attention of serious Christians. *After all, what was that thrill Fats Domino found on Blueberry Hill? Was it his first kiss, his first sexual experience, or did he just discover his belly button for the first time?*

Those seemingly innocent songs of the 50s reveal more than a hint of teasing sensuality and the restlessness of youth. Some were pretty bold in their pleading for love and their positive portrayals of young rebels. This music form had begun as a powerful expression of religious passion, devoted to the Almighty Father by faithful followers. But eventually it was adapted by the world to express a fervor for teenaged freedom and the irrepressible energy of young lust.

FROM GO-GOS TO GURUS

The imitation of black R&B music by whites took a new twist with the British invasion in 1964. America was introduced to British bands like Herman's Hermits, the Animals, the Yardbirds, the Hollies, the Dave Clark Five, and others. These groups often began with the mellow Mersey Beat sounds of Liverpool, but they gradually incorporated the sounds of American black artists. Some critics consider this period when rock and roll came to be known simply as rock.

Time would tell us that the most influential of these invaders would be the Beatles and the Rolling Stones. The Beatles created a stir with their looks and their candor. It wasn't that their hair was so long; it's just that they had the audacity to comb it down and let it hang there instead of slicking it back like everyone else. Something about their unique appearance and their cocky cockney comments made the girls swoon in ways that exceeded even the ecstasies previously brought about by Frankie (Sinatra) or Elvis (Presley).

Initially, the Beatles brought a sassy, yet romantic, image to rock and roll. The Stones brought a tougher, rebel, street image through this new form of British rock. So during the mid-60s the girls were typically fantasizing about John, Paul, George, and Ringo, while the guys were posing in front of their mirrors imitating the rawer rock stylings of the Rolling Stones.

The growth of rock music was not to be limited to a few British groups. The surfer sounds of Southern California were made popular across the country by the Beach Boys, Jan and Dean, the Safaris, the Ventures, and the Chantays (who gave us that 1963 instrumental anthem for the cowabunga crowd, "Pipeline").

The black sound of Motown (Detroit) came into its own with artists like the Supremes, the Miracles, and the Temptations. Folk music mixed relaxing rhythms and pointed challenges. Musicians like Simon and Garfunkel; Bob Dylan; Peter, Paul, and Mary; and others would eventually add some electricity (and bite) to their music to create folk-rock. Folk-oriented hootenannies were popular for a while, but gradually gave way to go-go clubs.

Teens tended to be self-preoccupied, lost in fantasies of cars, sock hops, and the misty-eyed pursuit of love. But by the late 60s, those fantasies were turned upside down by Vietnam, assassinations, hippies, gurus, and drugs. Vietnam brought an unescapable awareness that there was a bigger (and deadlier) world out there.

Here in America, battle lines were being drawn down the center of the generation gap, forcing people into one of two camps: over 30 or under 30. The youth movement evolved into its own subculture, with a unique look, dress, music, and language. The older generation was supposed to be into drinking martinis, making money, and spouting off about politics and big business. Those in the under-30 camp were into smoking grass (marijuana), making love (not war), and changing the world.

At the same time, music began to take on a different sound. Electronic instruments gave artists the ability to simulate the hazy confusion of their latest psychedelic drug trips. The piano and sax were being replaced as lead instruments by the electronic keyboard and the electric guitar—especially the guitar. What had been primarily a backup rhythm instrument since the big band days suddenly became the center of attention.

Jimi Hendrix did things with a guitar that no one had ever thought of before and so many have tried to copy since. He made an art out of feedback and electronic noise. He was joined by the likes of Jimmy Page, Jeff Beck, and Eric Clapton. The guitar god was born, and rock would never be the same.

As pent-up passions were channeled into the musical politics of persuasion, a whole generation was being schooled in the proper way to live and behave. Perceptive folk prophets like Joan Baez and Bob Dylan wrote sophisticated sonnets that required thought and evaluation. The combination of provocative lyrics and powerful music brought the flower children out of their smoke-filled reveries to a more militant urgency and an active commitment to their own survival. Rock music was becoming recognized as a significant social force. No longer was it considered an irritating, insignificant form of teen entertainment. It became the point of identity for a whole generation.

The newfound power of rock music opened the door for other movements which otherwise might have been lost in the shuffle of passing fads. For example, the music gave credence to the creative powers of drugs. Musicians and artists had been using drugs for decades, a practice that had always been considered exclusive to the eccentric and Bohemian lifestyles of the artistic community. But in the 60s, music and drugs became common property of "the people." The 1969 Woodstock festival is considered a tribute to this fact.

Musicians became teachers, bringing answers of peace and love. The only problem is that their instructions were faulty. As the music industry became more profitable, the musical educators were able to finance new and bolder ways to communicate "the truth." At first they contented themselves with exploring the electronic innovations that were being developed almost daily. But eventually they began to look for more than just a new sound. They began to travel the world looking for new styles, new instruments, and a new song. What they discovered was a host of answers to spiritual and personal questions they didn't even know they had!

The Beatles were among the first to take the magical mystery tour. After they began to be bored with an initial interest in the spiritual insights of LSD, they discovered Ravi Shankar and a stringed instrument called the sitar. Shankar tuned them in to the ways of eastern mysticism. The Beatles' trip to India to meet with the Maharishi

Mahesh Yogi was much publicized, as was John Lennon's subsequent disillusionment. After that trip, Lennon was never the same. Not even his new idol, Yoko Ono, could fully bring him out of his growing depression.

The Beatles were just four of the thousands of people seeking spiritual truth. Authors Seay and Neely contend that almost every significant rock artist or group reflects this spiritual search. The 1950s had been full of artists whose spiritual backgrounds influenced their music. But by the mid-60s, *Time* magazine declared that God was dead. The hippie generation of the 1960s and 1970s grew up without much of a serious religious heritage.

Many young people who had been brought up in a traditional Judeo-Christian culture abandoned their faith along with their childhood dreams. The American ideals of apple pie and "Leave It to Beaver" were shattered by the cruel reality of the war in Vietnam. The church had long since lost its influence.

But the need for spiritual answers still haunted this generation. No matter how far and how fast they flew, they kept seeking. Some looked to drug gurus like Timothy Leary, who told them they would find the truth within themselves through acid and other experimental chemicals. While looking for truth in an altered state of consciousness, many simply found themselves losing *any* sense of consciousness. Eastern mysticism offered such trips without the risk of chemical damage, and many began to follow. Still others experimented with ancient arts and occult religions that few had heard of before.

The Rolling Stones went through a period of dabbling in witchcraft under the tutelage of Anita Pallenburg. They documented their journey through Hell with albums like *Their Satanic Majesties Request* and *Beggars Banquet* (with the infamous song, "Sympathy for the Devil"). Many found it easy to believe the rumors that they had sold their souls to the devil.

The Grateful Dead sought answers in spiritism, Egyptology, and the practices of the Rosicrucians. Jim Morrison of The Doors had a well-documented obsession to know what was on "the other side," and he even married a witch in an occult ceremony just for the experience. (His obsessions with drugs and the afterlife resulted in his mysterious death in a bathtub in Paris.) The Moody Blues painted an almost prophetic picture of the New Age movement in their concept albums. The Who pursued the wisdom of Meher Baba. David Bowie proclaimed complete spiritual freedom through sexual ecstasy, a pursuit that continues to be popular today with artists like TLC and Madonna.

DAZED AND CONFUSED

With all this spiritual searching going on, no one paid much attention to the kooky ex-lion tamer, Anton La Vey, as he started his Church of Satan in San Francisco. But musical acts like Led Zeppelin, Black Sabbath, and Alice Cooper entered the 1970s being influenced by many of the same books that La Vey was studying. The promises of enlightenment and freedom through eastern mysticism gradually evolved into a celebration of the dark side by those who had grown comfortable in a dark world. By this time, the actual name of the devil was rarely mentioned—usually tongue in cheek, if at all. But the groundwork was laid for a veritable explosion of occult exploration in the 70s and 80s.

Although romantic pop music continued to be the mainstay of the American music scene in the 1970s, it began to take some strange twists and turns in that decade. Disco became the rage (and the predecessor to the rave of the 90s). The public got *Saturday Night Fever* from John Travolta, but the underground dance scene just got kinky as acts like Grace Jones performed with naked body builders and live tigers. By the early 80s a few desperate Disco Dannies were still "Staying Alive," but most of the rock world screamed that disco was dead.

The politics and spiritualism of the new guitar gods had found an outlet in what was known as album-oriented rock (AOR). Entire radio stations were created to represent groups whose subjects and music styles had become too complex for the average bubble-gum pop music fan to fathom. The music began to be referred to as "fusion-rock" as it fused rock with other musical styles like classical (Kansas; Jethro Tull; Yes; Genesis; Electric Light Orchestra; and Emerson, Lake, and Palmer), jazz (Chicago; and Blood, Sweat, and Tears), and even funk/soul (Earth, Wind, and Fire; and Sly and the Family Stone).

But eventually fusion gave way to confusion. The music, electronics, and recording techniques began to bog down in their own sense of self-importance. The power of primitive rock had become a victim of too much technology. Even the passions of romantic pop music were disappearing with mechanically correct tunes from the likes of Abba, the Bee Gees, and the Carpenters. The whole music industry was dying from this technical overkill. Record sales suffered a severe decline in the mid- to late-70s. It looked as if the rock giant was toppling under the weight of its own excess. The music press began to mourn the death of rock and roll. Some even sighed with relief.

While the rebellion of rock seemed to be ending in the United States, another kind of rebellion was beginning in England. Ironically enough, it was the cold despair of this rebellion that would put the fire back into the lifeless world of rock music. Severe economic instability hit Britain in the 1970s. Massive unemployment caused droves of young people to go on "the dole" (welfare). For many young people, it seemed as if the only alternatives to a life of welfare were to find a rich uncle or form a successful rock band. It was out of this socioeconomic situation that punk music was born.

This punk music was angry and critical. It lashed out against the institutions of schools, church, government, and anything else deemed unjust or hypocritical. In essence, punk music was protest music. But unlike protest songs of the decade before, it was not idealistic. It was nihilistic and fatalistic. It offered no solutions and painted the world as cold and colorless, dark and grim. Punkers rarely sang about a better world. They either didn't care or didn't believe it was possible.

Punkers were perhaps most critical of the record industry, which they saw as totally devoid of truth or passion. They felt that money, machines, and technology were manipulating mindless bands in producing an endless stream of romantic fluff to numb the minds of listless, apathetic listeners. They rebelled against that system by forming underground garage bands. They recorded their music on unsophisticated, store-bought tape recorders. They performed anywhere but the posh clubs. Signing a contract with an established record label was an act of treason to the cause. The goal was not to "make it big" or to change anything—but to simply express feelings. Punk music's only intent was to push its own disturbed version of "the truth" on an appalled public. It didn't matter whether anyone understood or not.

It is more than a bit ironic that the first punk group to seize widespread public attention was started as a hoax. An enterprising, but cynical, band manager named Malcolm McLaren was a modern-day P. T. Barnum. After managing the New York Dolls, an all-male band of crossdressers, he returned to London to run a fashion boutique. There he saw a punk movement creating a taste for the absurd, and he felt the timing was right to sell the ultimate music antiheroes.

His idea was to create a group that was the opposite of everything that made rock music popular. He hand-picked some young punks who loitered about his shop. They went by the names of Johnny Rotten (because he never brushed his teeth) and Sid Vicious. They hadn't much experience performing in public. They couldn't play their instruments well or carry a tune. They were unpleasant to look at and uncomfortable to be with. McLaren foisted this group on the public as the hottest rock phenomenon since the Beatles—and the public bought them. They called themselves the Sex Pistols.

The Sex Pistols took punk's antiestablishment stand to the limits. They popularized the concept of anarchy as a way of life, although many of their fans didn't really understand the concepts they were cheering for. They became a living testament to the bleak sense of fatalism and nihilism that punk espoused. And the band died as it lived—a senseless, foolish waste of potential.

When the band toured America, it created much controversy. A young American fan, Nancy Spungen, decided she was in love with bass player Sid Vicious. She even moved to England to be near him. Eventually he agreed to live with her. Since she was a heroin addict, Sid became one too. One day he awoke from a heroin haze and found his knife in Nancy's stomach. He couldn't remember how it got there. Nancy was dead and Sid was arrested. While out on bail, he died of a heroin overdose six weeks later. The case never went to court.

A movie was made of this story—a punk version of Romeo and Juliet—called *Sid and Nancy*. A reviewer in *Spin* magazine (6/86) summarized their lives this way: "Sid's whole identity was self-destruction. He was famous for dying. It's all he knew how to do. For Sid and Nancy, there was no more exciting way to be young than to die before they grew up." It's a summary of the punk movement that's tragically dead-on.

Chapter 6

TODAY'S MUSIC SCENE

●

*"For out of the overflow of the heart the
mouth speaks." (Matthew 12:34)*

In spite of its focus on death, the punk movement
brought life back to the music industry. Record companies got back to the basics. Rougher and rawer material
was sought. Lavish, overproduced songs were phased out
to make way for lean, stark productions and images.
Black became a popular color.

Another major factor in the music scene during the
1980s was MTV. With the proliferation of cable TV channels, an all-music channel was inevitable. Many predicted an early doom for this new concept when MTV
first aired in 1981. But the growing vitality of the rock
music industry gave muscle to the fledgling cable
concept.

Eventually MTV began to return the favor. It became
so popular that it was sometimes the sole factor in making or breaking a new artist. It changed fashion focus
from Hollywood chic to rock-and-roll outrageousness. It
shaped the way commercials were filmed. It brought the
ultimate personal recognition of rock stars into every
home, every day. No more staring at your favorite star
through binoculars at an annual concert. You could drool

over every nook and cranny of every hot body on MTV. You could even see the wrinkles in the eyes of aging band members. MTV helped fuel the fantasies of every rock-and-roll dreamer with bigger-than-life portraits.

The 1980s also reestablished the musical folk hero. Blue jeans and acoustic arrangements became accepted again. Bruce Springsteen, already recognized by music critics, became a popular favorite by the mid-80s. His rolled-up sleeves, jeans, and bandanna were the perfect point of identity for the mid-America, blue-collar crowd. This was no posturing glamour boy. He worked as hard at his concerts as his fans did at their jobs. He wrote about the beauty and sweat of America in a way people could relate to. He also brought socially-conscious lyrics back in vogue with songs about grass-roots Americans struggling over loss of farms and factory jobs, the forgotten veterans, and the love and suffering of the everyday American family. And he opened the door for neo-folk/pop artists such as Suzanne Vega, Tracy Chapman, R.E.M., and Natalie Merchant of 10,000 Maniacs.

Once again people were open to the power of music to promote awareness and change. Many of the monster groups of the mid-80s were the socially conscious ones. Live Aid helped make it hip to be charitable. Artists like U2 and Sting toured tirelessly for Amnesty International. John Cougar Mellencamp and Willie Nelson did the same for the farmers of America with Farm Aid.

This trend has produced a backhanded hypocrisy, however, in music industry rhetoric. Musicians proudly point to the power of music to produce social change for the good. They cite the hungry and homeless, apartheid, child abuse, starving children around the world—all these problems are being dealt with because music makes everyone more aware of these issues. On the other hand, when concerned critics and parents mention the negative images in music today, they are repeatedly told that there is no evidence that music causes adverse behavior in its listeners. *Are we really expected to believe that music can influence people for the good, but never for the bad?*

Such thinking is simply another myth promoted by the music industry's well-funded propaganda machine. Despite all the liberal rhetoric protesting the greed of the Reagan-era, the 80s was an extremely prosperous and profitable time for the entire entertainment industry, especially the music industry. By the end of the decade, sales of CDs and cassettes were bringing in a record $6.25 billion annually. And that figure does not reflect the sales of concert tickets, or the sales of band paraphernalia like T-shirts, hats, patches, and bumper stickers. And there is no sign of it stopping. Sales of CDs, cassettes, and music videos in 1994 topped $12 billion, a twenty percent increase over 1993 (*The Associated Press*, 2/16/95). Add to these figures the money being made by other types of entertainment—video rentals, TV, and movies (e.g., Americans paid $5.4 billion for movie tickets in 1994, a $200 million increase over 1993's record-setting pace)—and you begin to see just how much power the entertainment industry wields (*AP*, 1/6/95).

The entertainment industry is unquestionably one of the wealthiest and most powerful businesses in America today. They have a vested interest in influencing Americans as much as possible. Their bottom line depends on it. They need us to believe the myth that music doesn't influence anyone. They point to the dangerous power of religion and the government, because they don't want you to notice how dangerous and powerful *they* have become. They exert their tremendous influence on our culture in a way that should frighten us—they have convinced us to pay them to entertain us to death.

A NEW WAVE OF METAL MADNESS

Although punk kick-started the music industry, it was too abrasive to sell to the general public. In reaction to the angry guitars, some English artists began producing a synthesizer-based form of dance music that became known as new wave. This music was more melodic, danceable, and therefore, accessible. It found its heart in the foppish, makeup movement known as new romanticism with groups like Adam Ant, Boy George and his Culture Club, and Duran Duran. Eschewing the dressed-down simplicity of punk, new romantics tended toward dramatically colorful costumes and melodically emotive dance music. Boy George typified the movement with his gender-bender appearance, accented by lavish makeup, cross-dressing, and rag-doll fashions.

A darker side of this music emerged from clubs like the Batcave in London. Those artists who weren't angry enough to be punk or positive enough to be romantic, settled somewhere in between, in the dark music that came to be known as Gothic in England and death rock in America. A relatively obscure band called Bauhaus is usually given credit as the father of all things Gothic, but the most influential dark music artists of this period were Depeche Mode, the Cure, and Morrissey of the Smiths. The mood of the movement can best be summed up in Morrissey's outlook on life: "I've never been optimistic. I feel the light has gone out and that things just get progressively worse in every way. I'm bereft of spiritual solutions and I'm quite obsessed with death. I've gone through periods of intense envy for people who have died. I have a dramatic, unswayable, unavoidable obsession with death" (*New Music Express,* 2/20/88).

The philosophy of this music is known as nihilism, from the Latin word *nihil,* meaning "nothing." Nihilism insists that there is no particular point to our existence, and that expecting anything good, valuable, or lasting from this life is futile and absurd. We all meet the same meaningless end in death, after which there is only nothingness. When set to dance music, this philosophy teaches kids to resign themselves to their fate and learn to be happy about being hopeless.

Gradually, the music industry started using the term new wave for almost every new, young group or artist coming out. Such diverse styles as garage rock (a slightly less abrasive form of punk), quirky piano pop, synthesized dance music, neo-folk, rockabilly (e.g., the Stray Cats), and even zydeco were all being called new wave. The term was overused until it fell into disuse and became virtually meaningless. Besides, the music was being drowned out by the sheer volume of a new wave of heavy-metal maniacs.

In the 60s, artists like Jimi Hendrix and Led Zeppelin played psychedelic hard rock known as acid rock. In the 70s, hard rock was embellished with elaborate theatrical presentations by Alice Cooper and KISS. In the early 80s a new wave of metal bands began to burst on the scene with names like Judas Priest, Iron Maiden, and the Scorpions. The popularity of metal grew in the 1980s until there were at least three major types of metal from which to choose.

Black Metal

Some bands blended the shock-rock theatrics of Alice Cooper with the occult interests of Black Sabbath and Ozzie Osbourne to produce a style know as black metal. (Black metal is not a reference to race, but rather to black magic.) Initially, bands like W.A.S.P. and Lizzy Borden, and even early efforts by Twisted Sister and Motley Crue, were closer to the campy schlock rock of *Rocky Horror Picture Show* than any honest effort to reflect Satanism.

But as glam metal became more popular, some groups like Slayer, Danzig, and King Diamond began to take their Satanism more seriously.

Black metal concerts often featured skulls and skeletons, as well as simulated slashings and stabbings. Some groups pretended to drink blood or gnaw on some grisly bones. Others incorporated occult imagery, Satanic rites, and references to magic. Most of the lyrics were based on a mixture of occult literature and slasher films (like *Nightmare on Elm Street, Friday the 13th, Halloween,* and *The Texas Chainsaw Massacre*). Looking like rejects from a Friday-night freak show, they combined the grossest images from these movies with loud, driving rock to provide the ultimate in blood-curdling entertainment.

Fans are fond of pointing out that most of these bands rarely practice the occult in their personal lives. They merely capitalize on the style to sell more records. It's important to remind these fans that it really doesn't matter whether these bands actually pray to Satan or not. The greatest impact on their fans is during their concerts. When movie and magic special effects are displayed on stage with such dramatic flair, fans are encouraged to see it as harmless fun. If they become intrigued enough, they are more likely to explore and experiment with the occult or other violently demented practices on their own.

Glam Metal

The sensationalism of black metal led many churchgoers to believe that heavy metal was virtually synonymous with Satanism. But the most popular style of metal in the 80s had far more to do with sex than Satan. Glam metal grew out of the arena rock of the 70s carried by bands like Styx, Journey, and Foreigner, and gave birth to a new generation of pop metal bands like Def Leppard, Dokken, Motley Crue, Bon Jovi, Poison, Skid Row, and Guns N' Roses.

The sound was lighter, bouncier, and more melodic than the ponderous, pretentious metal of Iron Maiden or Black Sabbath. Early on, the look was characterized by brightly colored spandex, scarves, tons of hair spray on haystacks of hair, and layers of makeup on both men and women—a style of dress which could best be described as "the gay pirate" look. The festive dress, the accessible sounds, and the sexually romantic themes made this metal more appealing to the girls, which brought out the boys as well. This appeal to both men and women was one of the reasons that glam metal produced some of the biggest-selling albums on the charts in the mid-1980s.

As glam metal moved closer to its blues roots in the late 80s, the look was toned down to blue jeans, boots, and basic T-shirts. But the song remained the same. The key word was still "party." It sums up all the hedonistic pleasures the bands and fans could fancy. "Party" could mean any number of things: sex, drugs, alcohol, music, fun, dressing up, excitement, acceptance, romance, or escape from pressures or boredom. Musicians avoided openly encouraging young people to take illegal drugs or alcohol, while coyly condoning such practices simply by encouraging teens to party.

Of course, fans claim that they don't listen to the lyrics and that music doesn't affect them. But glam metal spoke louder than words, and the bands' lifestyles said plenty. Jon Bon Jovi said that he lived for only two things—to play rock and roll and to get drunk (*Graffiti*, 1/87). Poison's Brett Michaels claimed that the group toured with a computer listing of all their groupies—categorized by town, hair color, and the sexual activity they excelled at (*Rolling Stone*, 12/15/88). While driving drunk, Vince Neil of Motley Crüe killed a man and permanently handicapped two kids, but got off with a 30-day jail sentence and a fine (*Los Angeles Times*, 9/18/84). Axl Rose of Guns N' Roses confessed to regular cocaine and heroin use, but insisted he was too tough to become addicted (*RIP*, 4/89). You don't need to know all the lyrics of these bands to pick up on the messages they communicate.

Hardcore Metal

There was a time (in the early 80s) when punkers and stoners (heavy-metal fans) literally fought in the halls at high school over their music preferences. The stark hopelessness of punk didn't completely mesh with the melodramatic promises of power in the heavy-metal scene. Ultimately, however, the themes of punk and metal found common ground in thrash and speed metal, an aggressive style of rock blending chunky punk rhythms with the lightning leads of electric guitar. Bands like Metallica, Megadeth, and Anthrax started out in an underground relegated exclusively to macho-metal males. But as glam began to lose its glitter, more and more kids started looking for something harder and heavier. Once Metallica slowed the speed metal down on their album *And Justice For All* (and finally put a video on MTV), they found themselves where no one ever expected them—on the top of the charts.

The themes on thrash-metal albums can best be described as sixty-seven ways to die. Some lyrics (like Slayer's) are about the occult, but most focus on the gruesome details of death and dismemberment. Like punk, they usually get more political as the band members get older. At that point, the lyrics tend to be critical of the government, education, religion, and the family. There's little socially redeeming value in this music, but the appeal to young men is the danger, the excitement, and the power it helps them feel.

THE RISE OF RAP

Rap has probably been the biggest new music phenomenon in the past decade. The first real rap song is generally conceded to be "Rapper's Delight," by the Sugarhill Gang in 1979, but it was "The Message," by Grandmaster Flash (and the Furious Five) in 1982 that made the music industry realize that rap was marketable. It took hard rock, however, to bring rap to the white audience. In 1986, Run-DMC's version of Aerosmith's "Walk This Way" put rap on MTV and on the map.

Rap music started out as an East Coast phenomenon, with the braggin' and boastin' of street-corner B-boys like Kurtis Blow, Kool Moe Dee, and L.L. Cool J. Some rap fans defended this boasting as a way for young men to establish their identity and a sense of black pride, but it tends to simply be a self-centered substitute for true self-esteem. This became obvious as rap grew more offensive and deadly over time.

This viciousness was especially obvious in rappers' attitudes toward women. Referring to women as "ho's" (whores), rappers like Slick Rick advised young men to "Treat Her Like a Prostitute." The 2 Live Crew is so sexually explicit and demeaning, they've actually been prosecuted for producing pornographic albums. They not only describe women in the most crude and obscene terms, they illustrate their attitudes on stage in demeaning shows of simulated sex. Dr. Dre showed his lack of respect for women by throwing a female DJ through a door when she disagreed with him.

These negative and violent attitudes were not just directed at women. More and more gang members started getting into the rap attack. Rappers like N.W.A. (Niggaz Wit Attitude) and Ice-T glorified life on the urban streets with tales of drug deals, gang wars, sexual conquests, and the violent end that would come to anyone who dared to challenge their supremacy. Groups like Public Enemy began to reflect a militant black nationalism through the unity of the Nation of Islam. There is little in these calls to violence and revenge that resembles Christian values.

A REVOLUTION IN ROMANCE

Of course, not all kids are listening to the extreme, bizarre music on the edge. They listen to "normal" pop music, like the tunes that their parents grew up with. But we need to look closely at what constitutes "normal" in the world of romantic dance/pop music today. While some of the music may reflect an innocent romantic fluff, the trend over the last two decades has been toward depictions of graphic sexuality, multiple partners, adultery, and even kinky sex and sadomasochism. Very few modern love songs teach young listeners how to communicate, how to stay devoted to another person, or how to commit to a relationship for a lifetime. The message is simply that sex = love.

In other words, romance has been replaced by raging hormones, and falling in love is simply a matter of falling into bed. In 1966, the "wild thing" was the young lady who stirred the Troggs' passions; in 1988, Tone Loc reduced the wild thing to the sex act itself. "Let's fall in love forever" has been replaced by "Let's make love tonight." By the mid-80s, artists like Prince and Madonna were even stretching the boundaries of what "normal" sex was about, with graphic depictions of their desires and secret fantasies.

Making love gradually gave way to George Michael's demand "I Want Your Sex" in the late 80s. By the 90s, artists were asking for sex, not love, in such songs as Color Me Badd's "Sex Me Up," R. Kelly's "Sex Me," and

Montell Jordan's "I Just Wanna Get Laid." They don't even ask their partners anymore, they just snap their fingers and demand sex: "Do Me," demands Bell Biv Devoe, "Freak Me," echoes Shai ("freak" is frequently a none-too-subtle substitute for the "F-" word in R&B today). Much of this music comes in a derivative hip-hop style now known as new jack swing—a synthesis of rap and R&B.

Even the women are doing it in the 90s. Adina Howard makes kinky demands of a potential lover in "Freak Like Me" and explains, "I'm aggressive. There shouldn't be a double standard. Women should be just as aggressive as men" (*USA Today*, 5/9/95). No wonder even Christian kids no longer give a second thought to the implications of a song like Naughty By Nature's "Down With O.P.P." which blatantly declares that demanding sex with anyone at anytime (regardless of who they're married to) ought to be the norm.

This is definitely not in line with the Christian concept of loving, healthy relationships. The secular romantic myth says love is a swooning sensation—the right combination of soaring feelings, reeling senses, and hyperactive hormones is proof positive that you're in love. Teens are taught that they'll achieve this mythical feeling through the rush of passionate sex. Too often they believe the music, looking for love in all the wrong places, failing to understand that love lies in commitment and conformity to the character of Christ (1 Corinthians 13).

NOT MUCH IMPROVES IN THE 90S

A survey of music in the 1990s reveals that not all that much has changed about secular music except that it's getting darker, deadlier, and going deeper underground. The popularity of glam metal dwindled away by the end of the 80s. When Metallica softened speed metal to make it palatable to the masses, the real hard-core metalheads went underground. In America, the Tampa Bay area became the center of the death metal scene. Examples of death metal groups include Cannibal Corpse and Deicide. In England, the music became known as grind-core. Both styles try to be more gruesome and more brutal than speed and thrash metal, if that's possible.

As heavy metal became less glamorous and appealing, a host of other styles rushed in to fill the void. Searching for something they could relate to, a new generation of young teens in the early 90s found it in the revival of punk music. Younger teens related to pop-punk groups like Green Day and Offspring, while the older teens learned from old-school punks like Bad Religion or Henry Rollins, formerly of Black Flag.

As the fires of heavy metal died down, concerned parents and authorities found themselves facing a new musical menace in rap music. Most of the attention was focused on the violence and sexism of gangsta rap. Rappers were not satisfied to simply describe gang life on the urban streets—they glorified and encouraged it. Deciding to go further than defy authorities, rappers actually put out a call to kill cops (e.g., N.W.A.'s "F- the Police" in 1989, and Ice-T's "Cop Killer" in 1992). Newer rap artists didn't just rap about gangs and crime; they proved to be full-fledged participants, as more rappers went on trial like Tupac Shakur (rape), Snoopy Doggy Dogg (an accessory to murder), and Desean Cooper of Da Lench Mob (murder). By the mid-90s, the heat proved to be too much and rappers and record companies began backing away from the gangsta rap image, although not necessarily softening their lyrics.

Rap mirrored metal in other ways, as well. A rise in drug use since the days of "Just Say No" after the Reagan era can be linked with the popularity of marijuana among rappers. Tone Loc was one of the first in the late

80s to extol the virtues of grass in songs like "Mean Green" and "Chiba, Chiba." Dr. Dre left N.W.A. and put out a solo album called *The Chronic* (street slang for marijuana), praising the benefits of the wacky weed. The biggest proponents of the new freedom to smoke are Cypress Hill, who actually smoke grass on stage during their concerts. Rap also mirrored metal when groups like the Gravediggaz showed a growing fascination with horror and occult images and groups like Onyx were actually teaching fans to mosh. Moshing occurs in the pit at the front of a stage when kids are jumping, bouncing, and spinning among a mass of bodies.

Meanwhile, the hard-rock banner was carried on by a Seattle-based sound known as grunge rock. Grunge features overdriven guitars and dripping-with-lithium vocals for a sound that is hard, yet muddy (which is why it's sometimes referred to as "heavy muddle"). The better-known bands in this genre are Nirvana, Alice in Chains, Soundgarden, and Pearl Jam. Grunge came with a distinct fashion statement with its plaid shirts, baggy shorts, and grungy army boots. But grunge rock is mainly known for its manic-depressive themes and the high percentage of suicides and drug overdoses among its musicians.

Grunge was the bridge between the metal of the 80s and the alternative music of the 90s. As it often happens, when new wave became overmarketed, it went underground and regrouped, reemerging on college campuses across the country. College Radio catered to college students who preferred the post-punk sounds of modern rock groups like Kate Bush and R.E.M.

By the early 1990s, alternative music had become the new wave of popular music. And like new wave, alternative rock music has become a term that is so broad and inclusive, it's almost meaningless. Post-punk garage rock usually describes the harder-edge rock band whose music falls somewhere between punk and the Rolling Stones. It usually features a big guitar sound and cryptic lyrics about feeling lost in a big world. Early acts like Hüsker Dü and the Replacements have been replaced by newer bands like Soul Asylum and Dinosaur, Jr.

Modern rock can be used to describe the softer side of alternative rock. It includes the lighter jangly rock of the Breeders and R.E.M., as well as the orchestrated piano pop of quirky female artists like Kate Bush, Tori Amos, or Sam Phillips. The Celtic sound is also big in this arena, from the traditional sounds of Enya to the progressive pop/rock of the Cranberries. And there's the playful intellectualism of college-radio rock groups like They Might Be Giants, Camper Van Beethoven, and Weezer.

While Gothic music is back as an underground club phenomenon (show up at one these clubs and you'll think you stumbled into an Addams Family convention), it hadn't become a popular radio sound by the mid-90s. Its angry cousin, industrial music had, however. The stark, electronic rhythms are meant to reflect a heartless world in a cold computer age. The wailing vocals reflect the anguish of artists who have learned to express fifty-two shades of pain. While underground groups like Ministry, Skinny Puppy, and Front 242 represent this music well, Trent Reznor's Nine Inch Nails brought it to popular attention. Industrial is one brand of electronic dance music that's frequently heard at rave parties. As a flashback to the psychedelic 60s, rave music offers fans thumping dance rhythms and electronic overload, along with mood-altering drugs like Ecstacy and Euphoria, to give young people in the 90s another way to express the anarchy of their lives and the chaos in their souls.

The alternative scene is most visible at the Lollapalooza festivals. Perry Farrell (now of Porno for Pyros) originally conceived the festival as a farewell tour for his band Jane's Addiction. It was a bizarre collection of music, fashions, political statements, and perversions that made P. T. Barnum's sideshows look like an afternoon tea party. It did so well, the festival became an annual event. Tattoos and body piercing are an integral part of this alternative culture. In these circles, pierced ears and little rose tattoos are no longer sufficient. They plunge into full-body tattoos and the painful process of piercing every conceivable body part—including the genitals.

Alternative music may be popular, but it's not particularly healthy—mentally or spiritually. It tends to waver between the two extremes of pain and numbness. The "slacker" or "loser" mentality is an apathetic indifference—a numb attempt to ignore the pain and problems experienced in life. The other side dives deeply into their pain, exploring it, amplifying it, rehearsing it, massaging it, milking it for all it's worth. Generation X doesn't want you to tell them what to do; they want to find their own way. The problem is their music teaches them to resign themselves to the fact that there *is* no way out.

WHAT ABOUT THE FUTURE?

No one can accurately predict what's next on the musical horizon. It's obvious that pop/dance music will continue to be graphically suggestive and sexual. Young men will crave some kind of hard, outrageous rock style, whether its punk, metal, grunge, or some new hybrid rock. Political, social, and experimental religious themes will be around as long as they are amplified by the media in society.

Secular rock music will probably not disappear in the near future. The multibillion dollar industry is far too profitable. And it is naive for the church to engage in campaigns to "wipe rock music from the face of the earth." We cannot expect a sinful world to quit being sinful. If changes are to take place, they must begin with our own lives. Starting in our homes, we must begin to provide wise, biblical responses to the problem of offensive rock music. In our neighborhoods we must take a stand for morality, decency, and true spiritual values. The church must continue to offer suitable answers to the problems of the world. Rock music may never completely disappear, but its sinful appeal will fade and sales of violent and sexual entertainment will plummet in an honest and righteous nation (2 Chronicles 7:14).

"BUT IT DOESN'T AFFECT ME"

○

*"Don't associate with evil men; don't long for
their favors and gifts. Their kindness is a
trick; they want to use you as their pawn.
The delicious food they serve will turn sour in
your stomach and you will vomit it, and have
to take back your words of appreciation for
their 'kindness.'" (Proverbs 23:6-8, TLB)*

After a seminar at a beautiful summer camp, a young man approached me. He stood in stark contrast to the blue sky, green trees, and the rainbow of colors the other campers were wearing. He was dressed in black from head to foot—black shoes, black socks, baggy black pants, a black shirt with the collar buttoned, and another loose, silky black shirt over the other one—even though the weather was warm. His hair was dyed black and combed straight up, showing about an inch of brown roots. I didn't check, but I was willing to bet that even his underwear was black!

I greeted him before he could say a word. "Let me guess. Some of your favorite groups are The Cure, Depeche Mode, Siouxsie and the Banshees, Echo and the Bunnymen, Morrissey—groups like that."

The guy's jaw dropped. "That's right!" he exclaimed. "How did you know?"

"Just a lucky guess," I joked with a shrug.

He said, "I wanted to tell you that I liked your seminar, but I didn't like what you said about my favorite groups. I listen to them all the time, and they don't affect me."

I looked the young man up and down and asked, "Tell me. Does your mother dress you this way?"

He didn't seem to understand that I was teasing him. In fact, he was puzzled by my question. "Of course my mother doesn't dress me this way," he answered. "I dress me this way."

"No," I objected. "Your groups dress you this way. I'm not saying there's anything wrong with the way you're dressed. But if you don't see that your choice of music affects your choice of clothes, you're probably missing the connection between your music and your feelings, thoughts, values, beliefs, and many of your other choices in life."

He asked, "Are you saying that my music makes me dress this way?"

I replied, "No. Music doesn't hypnotize people and make them do things against their will. You and I know better than that. But we also know it's not fair to say that music has no influence at all. If you really like the music you listen to, it has the power to affect your thoughts, moods, and choices, and eventually even your behavior. You will see the effects at some point."

He was still reluctant to accept what I was saying. He said, "I suppose you're right. But I don't think my music will make me do anything bad. It's good music and I like it!" As he walked away, I just shook my head. Some people will perform some pretty amazing mental gymnastics to justify their music.

Perhaps you have had similar conversations. They can be exasperating, can't they? *Why are young people so blind to obvious truth? Why can't they see how influential their music can be? Why don't they change? Why are these discussions so difficult?*

It could be that we're missing the mark somehow. After years of talking to young people about music, I've discovered a couple of common roadblocks to progress in this area.

The first roadblock occurs because most adults use adult logic. As soon as many good Christian parents discover the immoral, foolish, and evil influences in today's music, they see the implications and feel the need to take immediate action. They proceed to explain the problems to their children and are amazed when the kids don't see the same obvious dangers.

Young people operate with a different logic. When I present facts verifying the evil side of rock music, most do not conclude: "Oh, my goodness! Look at those Satanic rock musicians doing such awful things. I guess I'd better stay away from all rock music!"

Teens don't generalize that way. They are at an age in which they test limits and tend to think in specifics. They are more likely to conclude: "Now I know which groups are bad. I'm sure glad he didn't mention any of *my* favorite groups. That must mean my music is okay."

This is one reason adults go around and around with young people on music. What seems logical and obvious to us doesn't make sense to them. They don't recognize the long-term effects the same way we do. So we need to be willing to be specific when we talk about rock groups and songs. *Have we done our homework? Can we take young people step by step through the spiritual and biblical points? Do we really know what the Bible says about this subject?* Of course, some teenagers don't want to sit still for such a discussion, but it's important to try.

The second roadblock occurs because we offer the right answer, but in response to the wrong question.

We've been led to believe that rock music problems can be solved by showing how evil the music really is. Once young people recognize the truth, they should change. But they're not changing. Why? *Isn't the music sinful, evil, and immoral?* Yes, in many cases it is. But we're not answering the real question in the minds of young people: *If the music doesn't affect me, what's the big deal?*

This is why young people believe it's okay to listen to whatever music pleases them. I hear all kinds of rationales: "Sure, some of the music is evil, but it doesn't affect anyone." "I don't listen to the lyrics." "The music affects some kids, but not me." "It doesn't affect my thinking; I just like the beat." "It's only entertainment. It can't harm you if it's fun." Young people honestly believe these things.

Christian parents have been addressing the issue of whether rock music is evil, and some have provided good, solid answers. But teens are more interested in questions like: *How does music affect me? Could it harm me? How can music possibly affect my spiritual growth? Can music influence me to do something I don't want to do?*

These are the issues we need to address. If we're going to make progress with our children, we have to answer their objections and questions, not ours.

Most young people refuse to believe that music influences them. They honestly don't see how it can, because they don't see an immediate impact on their lives. When they don't see dramatic, overnight changes in their lives, they assume that no changes are taking place at all.

I've literally had kids come up to me and say, "Look, I've listened to AC/DC three times today and I haven't killed anyone. See? The music doesn't affect me!" A 13-year-old girl once told me, "I listen to Madonna all the time and I haven't gone to bed with anyone."

This is how young people "prove" that their music is okay. They believe the music will never alter their values or change their thinking in any way. But music *does* affect them, and we need to be willing to show them how. We can suggest other ways to look at music's impact on their lives and provide answers that make sense to them. They may not want to hear what we have to say, but they are usually willing to listen if we are answering the right questions.

IN-FLIGHT INSTRUCTIONS

One day on an airplane a young man clambered aboard with an electric guitar slung over his shoulder. I noticed stickers with the logos of Black Sabbath, Ozzy Osbourne, Iron Maiden, and a number of other hard-rock bands on the guitar case. He stored it in the upper bin and took the aisle seat in my row.

On most of my trips I write articles, read and answer letters, or review new Christian music releases on my Walkman. I had a lot of work to do on this trip. I didn't want to talk, but I sensed God urging me to start a conversation with this young man. He was obviously involved in rock music, and I was perhaps the one individual in the whole world the Lord wanted next to him at that moment.

We exchanged pleasantries. He seemed like a nice guy, but to be truthful, I was hoping he would ignore me. Then I could explain to God that I had tried but he wasn't interested. The plane taxied to the runway and was soon airborne. When we reached our cruising altitude, I asked him, "Are you in a band?"

"Yeah, why?" he asked. He seemed to want to talk, so I decided to pursue it further.

"I saw the stickers on your guitar," I said, pointing to the upper bin. "Are you into hard rock?"

He responded enthusiastically and mentioned some of his favorite bands. I asked a few specific questions, and he was surprised I knew anything about those groups. I mentioned a few personnel changes and album titles only an aficionado would know. He began to look at me like one of his pals, "Hey, you into metal?"

Considering my age and "fortysomething" appearance, I was flattered. I mentioned that I was a music critic and published a Christian magazine that informed parents about the rock music scene. His face dropped. He thought I was setting him up to criticize his music, and his first response was to defend himself.

"Well," he said, "I like heavy metal, but it doesn't affect me."

"Oh, really?" I asked. "How do you know it doesn't?"

He squirmed a little. "Well, I enjoy listening to it, but I'm not a Satanist or anything like that."

"Ozzy [Osbourne] doesn't claim to be a Satanist either. It's just a gimmick to him," I said.

He nodded, apparently beginning to feel he was getting off the hook.

"So why would you think you would become a Satanist if you listened to Ozzy's music?"

"I just meant that his music doesn't make me kill small animals or beat up my little brother, or anything."

"Why do you listen to it?"

The young man shrugged. "Because it sounds so good."

It turned out that he had just finished the school term and was on his way to visit his father during summer vacation. "Tell me," I said, "do your teachers ever show movies in class?"

"Sure, sometimes."

"Do they use videos, television, slides, and audiotapes?"

"Yeah, they do."

84

"Do you know why?"

"It's more interesting. I know that."

"Those things are also good teaching tools," I pointed out. (After ten years as a schoolteacher, I knew that audiovisuals are among the best tools for education.) "Now, think. When you take that same tool out of your classroom and put it in your home, what do you call it?"

"I guess it's TV," he replied.

"How about MTV?" I asked.

"Yeah, I see what you're saying."

I continued, "So if it's instruction in the classroom, isn't it still instruction in the home? You're learning the values of your favorite groups, whether you realize it or not."

My young friend sat silently for a while. As we talked further, he began to see that music is more than entertainment. It is education, instruction, guidance, enlightenment, example, modeling, and more. I fished out my business card and a contemporary Christian music tape I was reviewing and handed them to him.

"Thanks," he said as I asked him to keep in touch. I felt that my young friend had gained a new perspective on his music and its effects. And I had learned a valuable lesson about being open to God's leading.

EDUCATION AS ENTERTAINMENT

At times, it is nearly impossible to make a distinction between entertainment and education. In 1988, the Parents' Music Resource Center (PMRC) released a video on rock music called *Rising to the Challenge.* The video begins with some footage of the classic educational program *Sesame Street* and makes some simple observations: We now have an entire generation raised and educated on TV. That generation grew up learning their

ABCs and reading their first words in an entertaining atmosphere of singable tunes, funny furry creatures, and special animation.

Then the narrator proposes a simple, but important question: *"When does a child stop learning from television?"* The answer is obvious. Children never stop learning, and television continues to be an influence as long as they watch.

Children's programming tries to prove that education can and should be fun. We have conditioned an entire generation to accept the fact that education and entertainment belong together. Many of the media today, especially television, justify content by insisting it has both educational and entertainment value. By design, the media attempts to affect people and change their lives.

But when it comes to music, this argument is supposedly no longer valid. The music industry tells us that music is only entertainment, and therefore it doesn't affect anyone. *But when did entertainment stop being educational? When do we stop learning from the media?*

Think this through, parents and teachers. *Would you invite a sexual pervert into your child's bedroom to teach him or her about sex?* Of course not. But if someone else adds a tune to that teaching, it becomes rock music.

Would you allow a Satanist into your house to explain his beliefs? No, yet that same philosophy may be accompanied by a melody and a regular beat, tucked among the albums in your child's rock music collection.

Would you invite Shirley MacLaine into your home to teach New Age philosophies and how to discover your previous lives? Musicians have turned out some very entertaining folk music and jazz based on those same beliefs.

We need to help our children understand these things. Music *does* affect listeners. Young people constantly look for answers to their most important questions: *What does it feel like to be in love? How should we treat our friends, our parents, ourselves? How does the world work? What can someone tell me about life and death? What is God like?* Their music educates them with answers that seem right (Proverbs 14:12).

It's not easy for young people to accept the fact that their music might be misleading them. The music is dynamic and exciting; education is boring. In their minds, one usually excludes the other. But the truth is that musicians have something they want to say (teach). At that point, music is no longer exclusively entertainment. It also becomes education. In fact, some musicians get downright preachy.

Normally, young people hate to be preached at. They don't like people who are oppressive and authoritarian, who shake fingers and shout commands. But when a secular "sermon" is put to rock music, young people suddenly begin to listen. When the performer is banging on a guitar instead of a pulpit, they can ignore the fact that he is actually preaching. Teenagers more readily accept a rock music message because they like the way it is preached.

This attitude is typical of the MTV generation. Young people are besieged with 24-hour music video channels. Rock music is filtered into movies, TV shows, and commercials. In search of entertainment, viewers forget that education comes with the package. The attempt to make education entertaining has also resulted in making entertainment educational. But instead of educating us in Judeo-Christian values, today's entertainment promotes promiscuous sex, violence, and selfishness.

ROCK-AND-ROLE MODELS

Parallel to the influence of rock music as an educational tool is the influence of musicians as role models.

Teenagers need heroes. They need flesh-and-blood people to show them that it is possible to overcome life's obstacles and be successful.

Traditionally, these heroes have included youth workers, ministers, scientists, sports figures, and other notable people. But for most young people today, heroes come from the media: TV, movies, and rock music. A recent poll of 2,000 students in grades 7–12 showed that 68 percent of them regarded an entertainer as a hero.

It's human nature to imitate our heroes. When young people find someone who is attractive and interesting, they often begin to model themselves after that person. Such imitation isn't always intentional, but it's commonplace.

Back in the days when KISS was wearing face paint, their fans would show up at their concerts in the same makeup. Wearing one white glove was once the rage among Michael Jackson fans. Madonna's wannabes dress (and act) just like her.

Many of today's biggest musicians admit they were influenced by their rock music heroes. Garth Brooks confesses that his concerts today are shaped by his love for KISS while he was growing up. Trent Reznor of Nine Inch Nails (whose look has also been influenced by KISS) admits that listening to The Cure and Pink Floyd is what helped him get through his teen years. "It made me feel almost normal, hearing someone who was more depressed than me" (*RIP*, 3/92). Artist after artist confesses that music was his best friend, sometimes his only friend, while he was growing up. If it affects famous people like this, what makes us think that it isn't affecting the everyday kids in our neighborhood or our home?

Tragically, the consequences of imitating today's rock music heroes grow more deadly as the music grows more hopeless and nihilistic. For instance, Pearl Jam's MTV video hit "Jeremy" depicted a young boy who committed suicide in his classroom for show-and-tell because, "Daddy didn't give attention/To the fact that Mommy didn't care." (*Blade,* 5/15/94). The video inspired several copycat suicides, including a 10-year-old boy who shot himself on the steps of his elementary school in Los Angeles (*AP,* 4/17/94). After Kurt Cobain of Nirvana committed suicide with a shotgun, a number of teens across the country killed themselves in sympathy (*Los Angeles Times,* 10/19/94).

Young people *will* imitate those they admire. It's just that they don't always pick the most admirable people to imitate. They want to believe that their behavior is solely their own choice and their own original idea. But it's pretty hard to miss the connection between rock fans who dress like their favorite band or artist. Copying their heroes may be as harmless as dressing in black or as dangerous as committing suicide, but one way or the other, adolescents *will* imitate their heroes. That's why it's so important to choose the right heroes.

You may get some resistance from your children when you discuss these ideas. It's not that they won't see the sense in what you're saying. They can admit that the media is both entertaining and educational. They'll confess to admiring some of their rock heroes. But they may desperately try to cling to the idea that the music isn't really affecting them.

They offer a million excuses: *The music isn't that bad. They know where to draw the line. They can control themselves. They don't worship the music or the musicians. They don't see any real changes in their behavior. Rock music may affect some kids, but it doesn't affect them.*

When you hear all these arguments, hold your ground. The truth is that young people are buying just about every product and philosophy the music world is trying to sell them. While you don't want to be over-bearing or closed-minded, you may be the only person who challenges them to consider some hard truths. In the long run, most young people will be glad you did. ♩

Chapter 8

THE MEDIUM IS THE MESSAGE

●

"Avoid godless chatter, because those who indulge in it will become more and more ungodly. Their teaching will spread like gangrene." (2 Timothy 2:16, 17a)

Teens like to believe they are exceptions to most any rule. They feel that they are invulnerable, even immortal, and nothing devastating can happen to them. They conclude that since they feel the same today as they did yesterday, no drastic changes could be taking place.

So don't expect young people to immediately embrace the idea that their music might be damaging to them. But piece by piece, we can offer evidence that music *does* affect them.

For example, in 1986, the Beastie Boys released *Licensed to Ill.* One reviewer reported that the album "delivered school yard brays about the wonderfulness of shooting people in the head, getting drunk, using drugs, smoking, treating women as sex objects, pillaging, and theft. But hey, it's all a joke, we're told. So don't worry. (The kids all get the joke, right?) That's why Heublein reports sales of its Brass Monkey hooch have doubled since the Beasties' song extolled it" (*Spin*, 2/87).

The reviewer mentions a song on the album called "Brass Monkey," which refers to a brand of alcohol by that name. This song, though a "joke" to the band, was certainly no joke to the sales of the liquor company. (But perhaps they should take a closer look at the consumers of their product. The Beastie Boys' peak audience is between 12 and 16 years old.)

The correlation between the song and the increase in sales is obvious. Even Heublein admitted it. So it's important to recognize more than a casual connection between music and the products it extols. *How can the record industry claim not to affect anyone when it can sell alcohol without even trying?*

COMMERCIAL SUCCESS: DOLLARS TO DONUTS

With this example in mind, we need to consider a simple question: *What's the difference between a rock video and many of today's television commercials?* Are you still thinking? Are you stumped?

The answer is that there is little or no difference. If you watch MTV for awhile, you'll see how video producers combine a rock song with a barrage of quick visual images. Look at some of the more popular TV ads and see how the same methods are used. MTV, VH1, and other video channels deliberately choose commercials that reflect the look and sound of their videos. They don't want the viewer to feel his entertainment is being interrupted. In fact, the primary difference between a music video and a music-based TV ad is the length. Commercials are 15 to 60 seconds in length, while a rock video is usually 3 to 5 minutes.

These facts should make us stop and think. Research shows that music-based commercials are very effective in selling their products, even in 30-second segments. So think of the potential of music videos. They have a "product" to sell (values and philosophies) and they have much more time to capture our attention. The question isn't whether rock music can influence us. It does. The real question is: *How does the music affect us and what products is it trying to sell?*

A few years ago in California, a series of TV ads promoted a chain of donut shops. The viewers saw luscious, tantalizing donuts on the screen while overhearing Ralph and Norma, who appeared to be seeing the donuts at the same time. They were tempted by the mouth-watering treats—some smothered in cherries, some dipped in scrumptious chocolate, and others decorated with party candies. In the background Norma whined, "Look, Ralph, there's that donut commercial again."

"Norma," Ralph answered in the background, "I can't look at those donuts. You know I can't stand it. I'm weak-willed. I won't be able to resist."

"Oh, yes," Norma answered, "they've got those donuts, Ralph. Look at them. The lemon-filled donuts, the cherries dripping all over, and your favorite, Ralph, the rainbow sprinkles."

Ralph couldn't resist any longer. He started to drool, ran for the car keys, and roared off to the donut shop.

At my seminars I often ask the audience how many of them have Ralph's response to that commercial—jumping right up and buying a donut every time they see a donut commercial. No one raises a hand. Nobody wants to admit to being a slave to their salivary glands!

Then I ask a second question: "How many, if you had seen those donut commercials, would think, 'Hmmm. That looks pretty good. Sometime I'd like to try one of those donuts'"? A lot more people raise their hands. The commercials are often so appealing that viewers will usually try one if the opportunity presents itself.

Then I ask one more question: "How many of you, if the donut commercial were on, would think about donuts?" Almost everyone raises a hand. Of course, as long as someone is sitting there watching the not-so-subtle display of tantalizing donuts, he or she can't help but think about donuts. We're naturally going to think about what we're viewing at that moment.

Now think about the videos on MTV. Many have very sexy women with beautiful, long hair, wearing very tight skirts. They are seen lying all over cars, dancing in wet T-shirts, or standing in sexy poses. Some are naked, but you can never quite see everything. A lot of sexual posturing is going on in these videos. *What is being advertised? And why go to all this effort if not to affect someone?*

In my seminars, I ask the males in the audience, "Guys, how many of you watch a sexy video, and as soon as it's over, call your girlfriend, and invite her over to hug and smooch and get all sweaty?" I don't actually ask for a show of hands, because no one wants to admit to that kind of response. Besides, most people don't react immediately to those videos. No one believes that watching a sexy video will make anyone get pregnant or get raped—any more than watching a donut commercial makes people jump right up and buy donuts.

Then I ask a second question: "How many of you guys watch a sexy video and daydream about being with your girlfriend—dancing with her or going out on a date? Even if you didn't do anything about it, have you had those longings?" A lot of young men begin to nod and grin at that point, saying, "Yeah, but of course, I would never do anything wrong."

Then I ask a third question: "How many of you, while watching a sexy video, are thinking about sex and romance? How many of you have thoughts that contradict Jesus' words about Christian relationships?"

The audience usually grows silent. Nobody moves or says a thing. Nearly every person would raise his hand if he were being honest. When people look at donuts, they're going to think about donuts. When they watch a continuous stream of sensuous images, they're going to have sensual thoughts.

NO DEPOSIT, NO RETURN

While many youth see the point we're making here, they still resist making a personal application. They are convinced they aren't going to turn into perverts just because they tune into MTV once in a while. Just thinking about sex and romance isn't going to make them *do* anything. Music just doesn't affect them that way.

But can they be sure? *Is there truly no effect on the person's spiritual life?* Remember, Proverbs 23:7 says, "For as [a man] thinks in his heart, so is he" (*NKJV*). Let's think a little more about the influence of commercials (and music videos).

Why do American businesses spend so much money on advertising? For instance, did you know that *Seinfeld* got the highest advertising fees of any prime-time TV program in 1994? They charged advertisers $390,000 for every 30-second spot run on that show (*TV Guide*, 10/15/94). And McDonald's spent $1 million for every 30-second commercial spot they aired on the Super Bowl in 1995 (*USA Today*, 1/9/95)—it was only $40,000 per commercial in 1967. That's a lot of french fries! Why would McDonald's spend that kind of money if advertising didn't work? For that matter, where would they get that kind of money if advertising didn't work? All the available research shows that it's money well spent. Every dollar spent on advertising comes back in money spent on burgers and fries—and then some!

Advertising seeks to influence us, and advertisers know how the human mind works. They use all of that knowledge to try to persuade us to buy their clients' products. Commercials aren't generally designed to make the average person respond immediately in a direct, overnight, sensational manner. They are designed first and foremost to capture our attention and plant information in our minds about the benefits of the products. Later, when the circumstances are right, we're more likely to buy what they are selling. When we pass a donut shop with a few dollars in our pocket, we are much more likely to stop if we've seen their ads than if we had never been exposed to that suggestion.

The second goal of the advertiser is to get us to feel good about the product. This is why so many TV commercials use rock music in the background. Advertisers know that this music evokes positive thoughts for the target audience. If they can link their products with positive associations in the minds of their viewers, they know we're likely to buy their product.

A casual survey of TV commercials will reveal a large percentage of advertisers who use popular rock music to present their products. And if you identify the era the song comes from, you can usually tell who the target audience is. Those who want the attention of the baby boomer crowd will use 50s, 60s, and occasionally 70s music; those who are selling teenage and college products use 80s and 90s music. Since people have a positive association with certain songs, advertisers have learned to better their chances of influencing potential buyers.

The same principles apply to rock music cassettes, CDs, and videos. The more we listen to a certain artist, the more likely we are to buy into his "commercial"—the message he is trying to "sell." We may like the melody; we may like the beat; we may think the artist is cute; we may have an exciting time at the concert. Any of these factors may increase the likelihood that we will perceive the music and its message as a positive thing. Eventually, we may begin to like everything that goes with the music—even the immorality, selfishness, or violence that it describes. And later, when the circumstances are right, we're more likely to act on this message.

So when a 13-year-old girl justifies listening to Madonna's music because she hasn't gone to bed with anyone, be aware that she has simply not acted on any of those messages yet. But what about later, when she gets boyfriends who are more handsome (or aggressive)? When she's older and her sexual drives are stronger? When she's free from her parents' influence and has more opportunity? At that point, which commercial is she more likely to buy into: Madonna's, or the church's?

To be truthful, she probably has much stronger feelings and associations connected with Madonna's music than with church, so she is more likely to act on Madonna's suggestions. By the time she does, she may not even remember where those ideas came from. She may believe that the choices are her own. After a few years of listening to those secular music "commercials" for two to six hours a day (if she's average), she probably won't even realize how she is being conditioned.

The regular influence of music works like a commercial to produce some gradual, and potentially damaging, effects. But there are immediate effects as well. Entertaining ourselves with ungodly philosophies will immediately begin to challenge our faith and joy. It creates serious doubts about the basic elements of the Christian life: *Am I really saved? Does God really love me? Does God hear my prayers? Are my sins really forgiven?*

The minute we take an interest in what the secular world is selling us, we begin to lose interest in what Christ offers. No one can be committed to both ideas at the same time (Matthew 6:24). Entertainers don't usually tell their fans to forget about Jesus or to doubt their salvation, but many suggest that rock provides as much satisfaction as anyone could want from life.

Musicians don't always come right out and say, "Christianity is stupid and boring." Instead, a group like Aerosmith tells kids that real excitement comes from having sex in an elevator. Bands like Rage Against the Machine and Nine Inch Nails are telling them that biblical morality is stupid and outdated. Bands from Bon Jovi to Jackyl, and rappers from The 2 Live Crew to Dr. Dre tell their male fans that a woman's only purpose in life is to please them sexually. And female artists from Madonna to Adina Howard, from Liz Phair to Courtney Love, and from Salt-n-Pepa to TLC are telling their young female fans to be more aggressive about pursuing boys for sex. Today's musicians promote sexual activity in a way that makes it look attractive, exciting, fun, natural—what everyone is doing all the time! That's their commercial.

Young Christians are immediately faced with a choice. Which will they choose—Jesus' message or rock music's message? Can't they choose both? No, because God didn't design our minds (and hearts) that way.

Research has proven that we cannot consciously hold two opposing ideas about the same subject in our minds at once. In psychology, this is known as cognitive dissonance. When faced with such a dilemma, we automatically reject one or try to somehow force an agreement of the two thoughts. People react to the idea of opposing "truths" by justifying, rationalizing, or rejecting parts of the opposing ideas in order to resolve the conflict.

Therefore, when Christians are faced with commercials selling philosophies that contradict Jesus' teachings, we immediately begin to work at resolving the contradictions. That's why Jesus stresses that we cannot serve two masters. We will hate one and love the other. We cannot live with that mental, emotional, and spiritual conflict. We must resolve it one way or the other.

Over time, this can create a complete rejection of God and His Word. After listening to the world's truth presented in today's music, average young Christians will begin to justify their listening habits. Subconsciously they begin to think, *"I can't believe that a loving God would want me to deny happiness and physical fulfillment with my girlfriend/boyfriend."* Later they think, *"I can't believe that a loving God would want to deny me physical fulfillment whenever I want it."* Still later it becomes, *"I can't believe that a loving God would...* (fill in the blank)." Finally, it's simply, *"I can't believe in a loving God."*

How does someone turn from following Christ to a life of immorality? One step at a time. Remember, the Bible doesn't say that you'll become a sexual pervert if you entertain yourself with sexual perverts. But it does say you will undermine your faith and joy if you continue to entertain yourself with the empty philosophies of this world which are against biblical values.

How is your faith and joy? With what are you entertaining yourself? Does it conflict with what Jesus teaches? How are you going to resolve the contradiction?

FALL OF A PRINCESS

Step by step, day after day, we are being educated about "the way life should be" from the world's point of view. We are besieged with "commercials" advertising the benefits of immoral living, selfish choices, and destructive behavior. And it's working. Church after church and family after family report that their young people are struggling and failing in all the same ways as young people without Christ.

Personally, I would even go as far as to say that secular music and other forms of entertainment are destroying Christianity! Before you think that I have gone too far, think this through. How do you destroy Christianity? By burning down churches? Christian schools and colleges?

Bibles? How about burning Christians? No! Those have all been tried before and have only succeeded in making the church stronger.

You destroy Christianity by destroying a Christian's morals. Moral values are the outer signs of an inner spiritual condition. The Bible teaches that if we are strong spiritually, we will exemplify strong morality. This is why we are commanded to "Flee the evil desires of youth" (2 Timothy 2:22). If our moral values are destroyed, our spiritual values will also be destroyed. If we compromise our morals, we also compromise our Christian witness.

A question I like to ask my audiences is: "Would you attend a church if you knew the pastor was a sexual pervert?" I've never heard an audience say yes. They all know instinctively that they could never learn spiritual truth from a man whose morals are corrupted. Yet many of today's professing Christians are having their moral foundations destroyed by gradual (but persistent) erosion caused by their choice of entertainment. We are becoming a nation that is being entertained to death—spiritually. Let me share a painful personal example.

Many years ago when I was a Christian high-school teacher, one of my students was an adorable young lady, gifted with both beauty and intelligence. She was a popular cheerleader who was elected Homecoming Princess. It was expected she would excel in whatever endeavor she undertook. But she had an inner struggle—she did not want to live for Jesus Christ.

When I counseled her about dating non-Christian guys, she said, "Oh, I can date whomever I want to for now. When I get older, I'll live for Jesus. I just want to have some fun and do my own thing for awhile."

I knew she was heading for trouble, but I was unable to get through to her. I told her, "God has a special plan for your life, but you're going to experience a lot of heartaches because of this attitude. I want you to remember that I'll always care. Please contact me when you are ready to follow Jesus Christ."

She laughed and said, "Don't worry about me. I'll be okay. I just want to live a little first." Her implication was that you can't enjoy life if you are living for Christ.

Through her parents, I kept track of her life. She graduated from college, married, had a baby, got a divorce, and lost custody of her child. I hadn't talked with her since her wedding, but I prayed for her whenever I thought of our counseling sessions. Eleven years after her high-school graduation (and seven years since I had last spoken with her), she phoned me, wanting to talk. Even though I hadn't seen her since her wedding, she'd remembered that I would always care. And I did.

She was still cute, but her nose and cheeks were a little bloodshot. By this time she was an alcoholic and a heavy user of drugs. (She had lost custody of her child because she had been declared an unfit mother.) The guy she'd been living with for several weeks had tired of her and had thrown her out. She was at the end of her rope.

As she poured out the story of her immoral activities, I was dying inside. Although her attitude was matter-of-fact and emotionless, I could feel tears well up in my eyes. Where was the sweet, innocent girl I had known? I have found through experience to be blunt in my counseling. When I felt I couldn't take any more, I looked her straight in the face and asked, "Have you no shame?"

"No," she said. "None."

I didn't realize until later that her life reflected a song called "On Fire," from Madonna's first album. Madonna sings in one of the verses:

"On my back, on my knees,
I'll do anything to please.
I'm not the same, *I have no shame*,
'Cause I'm on fire,
On fire for your love." (emphasis mine)

I assured my friend of God's love and His offer of salvation for her. After many hours of counseling, I saw my former student finally surrender and let Jesus take charge of her life. How much better it would have been if she had responded to His call in high school! How different her life might have been if she hadn't bought the package of worldly glitter. I'm not saying that she fell because she listened to rock music. But I can say for certain that the music she idolized sold the lie that sex is love. She got what she desired. Only too late did she discover that it offered only emptiness and failure.

Back in the days when I was burning records, I wish I had known what I know now. Maybe I could have been able to explain the importance of her choices in terms she understood. Maybe I could have shown her how she had bought into the commercial of glamour and sexuality. Maybe I could have approached her in a nondefensive way. Maybe I could have helped save her the pain and agony she endured.

Maybe not. Not everyone will understand or respond. Some are going to be prodigals. Some are never going to listen. I just wish I had answered the question "Does the music affect you?" more effectively. I pray that we can understand this approach and be more effective with our kids. From this point on, perhaps we can save some of our future homecoming princesses and other young people from going down this same path.

Yes, music *does* influence kids. It educates them. It models philosophies and behavior through their heroes. It influences them like a commercial. If we can get young people to see this, we have a chance of helping them grow into strong Christians with genuine faith and joy. But these principles don't apply just to our children. Before we go any further, we need to turn the spotlight of truth on ourselves. ▪

Chapter 9

"IF ONLY THEY'D LISTEN TO MY MUSIC"

●

*"Set an example for the believers in speech,
in life, in love, in faith and in purity."
(1 Timothy 4:12)*

Back in my college days in the 1960s, I enjoyed pointing out the hypocrisies of "the establishment." A common picture of the time was of a businessman, martini in hand, barging into his hippie son's room to lecture on the evils of smoking marijuana. As a young man, I immediately saw through that double standard. If our drugs were wrong, why weren't *their* drugs? I never understood why the older generation couldn't see the contradiction.

Today it's much the same when it comes to the issue of music. Young people may not be as experienced as adults in the ways of the world or the ways of the Lord, but they can quickly see through contradictions and hypocrisy. Adults who only pretend to be interested or knowledgeable are easily spotted.

DISCOURAGING WORDS

Young people frequently point out a new contradiction—the issue of "their" music vs. "our" music. The issue is never as poignant as when parents (mostly fathers) tell me, "Al, I'm so glad you're talking about this disgusting rock music, with its booze, violence, and adultery. Why can't my kids listen to country music? Country music is God's music."

That assessment of country music couldn't be further from the truth. If you compare the themes of today's country music and today's rock music, you will find hardly any difference. If you took away the booze, the fights, the adultery, and the self-pity from country music, there would be nothing left to sing about except your mama and my pickup truck!

Country music wasn't always that way. Out on the range of yesteryear, life was simple and tame, and so was the music. There seldom was heard a discouraging word and the skies were not cloudy all day.

Not so today. Those skies—and the songs that describe them— have become polluted by the immorality of country-western songwriters. Cowboy Bob has parked his horse at the saloon and is getting drunk and beating his wife and kids. The sheriff is cheating on his wife; the schoolteacher is molesting little girls; and the preacher has run off with the prostitute. Dances are for hustling honky-tonk women. Bars are for crying in your beer. Families are a convenience to come home to, if they don't cramp a guy's style. And God is pictured as looking benignly on all this behavior.

Some parents grew up with southern gospel music and mistakenly believe that most country-western songs are pretty much the same. They tend to defend country music because they grew up with it. But wait a minute! *Isn't that the same reason many of their children use to defend their music?* It's what they've grown up with, what their friends listen to, and what they're comfortable with.

Some parents seem to be unaware that empty philosophies can be passed along by musical means other than hard rock. Young people see right through this contradiction, even if their parents can't. The truth is, both country-western and secular rock music can undermine a believer's faith and joy by proclaiming empty philosophies of this world built on men's thoughts and ideas instead of on what Christ has taught.

Dads, be careful not to yield to the temptation to take the easy way out as head of the household. The "Do as I say, not as I do" approach is not biblical. A Christian father devoted to the principles of Scripture needs to practice what he preaches. If he asks his son to remove immoral music from his life, Dad should first evaluate whether he has immoral music, TV programs, movies, or magazines in his own life. If he is struggling in this area, his children are likely to struggle as well. Before Dad can demand that his children deal with their music, he must first be willing to obey God's direction to deal with the media in his *own* life.

MELLOW LUST

When I talk about rock music in my seminars, I see moms poke their children in the ribs as if to say, "Are you listening?" And when I get to country music, Mom might jab her husband's ribs, saying, "Are you paying attention, here?" But when I discuss the Barry Manilow/Michael Bolton style of pop music, she mutters, "Now he's gone too far." She may even feel like getting up and walking out, but she's being held firmly in place by the elbows of Dad and the kids! Now she knows how her kids felt during the other part of the seminar. As uncomfortable as it may be, moms, just like everyone else, need to take a serious look at their entertainment. If moms think pop music is always safe to listen to, just because it's mellow, then they need to listen a little harder.

One of the clearest examples of what I call "mellow lust" was a song by Neil Diamond called "Desirée." This song spells out in detail how Desirée, a woman in her thirties, taught a 17-year-old boy how to be a man on a hot summer night in the backseat of a car.

What a lie! Desirée did not teach him how to be a man. She taught him how to have sex. Animals have sex, but that doesn't make them men. Sleeping with a woman doesn't make someone a man any more than sleeping in a garage makes him a car. This song teaches a philosophy of life contrary to biblical principles. Watch out! Just because it's mellow doesn't mean it's moral.

In my day, Donna Summer moaned sexually to a disco beat. Today Janet Jackson does the same thing during her song "The Body That Loves You," from her album *janet* (1993). Today the clearest examples of mellow lust are found in the R&B section: Mary J. Blige, R. Kelly, Shai, Silk, Jodeci, etc. But it's the music that makes this lust mellow, not the lyrics. The lyrics for some of these groups are as blatantly sexual as anything put out by The 2 Live Crew or any gangsta rapper. (Would you consider these lyrics by Mary J. Blige, "Come into my bedroom honey/What I got will make you spend money" subtle and romantic? Many kids do.)

But don't let the mellow music fool you. Too often parents fall for the obvious. When they find their children listening to a wild romp like "Love in an Elevator," by Aerosmith, they may be tempted to go ballistic. To soothe their nerves, they may go and listen to Barry Manilow and Michael Bolton, pleading for their lovers to stay the night. In God's sight, what's the difference between Aerosmith having wild sex with an unmarried partner in an elevator and Barry or Michael having mellow sex with an unmarried partner in his apartment? Technically, the only difference is about thirty feet—from the elevator door to the apartment door! Immoral behavior being presented in a soft, seductive package is no less sinful than the raw sound of wild sex or rebellion. In God's eyes, sin is sin.

One more time: God says that if we choose to entertain ourselves with philosophies that are against biblical values, we'll struggle with our faith and joy. This is true whether those philosophies take the form of easy listening or hard rock. *Parent, how is your faith in Jesus Christ and the joy of your salvation? Are you struggling in your marriage? Are you just going through the motions of Christianity?* Don't allow empty philosophies to undermine your spiritual walk with God.

THE COMPROMISE CALLED TV

Parents may also need to take inventory of their television viewing habits before they try to communicate to a child about rock music. Some parents even yell at their kids such things as, "Shut off that music! I'm trying to watch *NYPD Blue!*" This is another contradiction that is transparent to children.

What is the difference in the morality of many television programs and the morality of most rock music? Television seems to be a more acceptable medium for entertainment and education, so we tend to excuse it. But there is often no difference at all.

If someone spent his evenings prowling through your neighborhood, roaming from house to house, peeking into bedroom windows watching couples have sex, and describing his voyeuristic exploits to friends as a means of mental relaxation, you would likely consider this person a pervert. Right? Yet isn't that what television makes of us? It takes our mind's eye into bedroom after bedroom, night after night, channel after channel. How many times do we sit and watch immoral scenes and programs, justifying them by saying the immorality is only secondary to the real story? After all, it's simply entertainment. It doesn't affect us, right?

I can't speak for women, because at no time in my life was I ever a woman. But I believe I can speak for the normal male (taking into account that I'm from Southern California). I have to think that any man who says he can watch a steamy sexual encounter on television without being encouraged to lust is fooling himself.

Those scenes are added to TV programming so the viewers will lust. And since lust is stimulating, the program will be thought of as stimulating, which increases its audience size. However, the Bible clearly states that we are to take every thought captive to the glory of God (2 Corinthians 10:5). And rather than stimulate our lusts, we are to flee them (2 Timothy 2:22).

When Christians compromise their convictions, they send a message to their kids that it's okay. When these parents face an extreme kind of music, they may panic, lecture, and try to redirect their children's entertainment. But if parents have not looked critically at their own entertainment, they have little room to criticize.

We have no basis on which to manage our children's lives if we haven't managed our own lives according to Scripture. A mature Christian should be one who "manages his own household well, keeping his children under control with all dignity" (1 Timothy 3:4, *NASB*). That does not mean that the parent should control the members of his family with an iron fist. Rather, a Christian parent should manage his own life so well that his children can see how to live as Christians.

Much research has been done on the negative influence of television on the family. Don't write it off, thinking that your family is the exception. If parents aren't willing to examine and clean up their own habits, they can't expect their children to be obedient to their wishes.

We cannot say, "We're adults; we can handle immorality." If you can show me one family that can, I'll show you a hundred who have tried and failed. As responsible Christian adults, we have to be positive examples of what we want our children to grow up to be.

A CLEAN ACT

I heard about a test given to mental patients at a sanitarium to see if they were well enough to be released. The inmate is placed in a room in which the sink is plugged and the faucet is on full blast. He is given a bucket and mop and is told to mop up the water. If he doesn't turn off the faucet before starting to mop the floor, he is judged unfit to reenter society.

We face similar tests in our own lives. We won't be ready to deal with our children until we first deal with our own faucet—the media, which pours so much junk into our homes. As parents, we need to examine our own approach to television, movies, videos, music, books, and magazines to see what kind of messages we allow into our lives. If we haven't "shut off the faucet" to immoral influences, we're just going to keep mopping the floor of our children's lives, because *theirs* will be a spillover of our own.

Are you willing as a family to examine all the entertainment currently in your home? Are you doing anything that sends a contradictory message—perhaps saying one thing and doing another? Are you willing to let your children discuss areas they feel you have compromised? If you are ready to talk about these problems, you are setting the stage for helping your children grow strong in their Christian lives.

THE SACRIFICE

Honest parental self-examination requires some sacrifices and the willingness to answer some tough questions.

Sometimes it is hard for parents to live up to Jesus' simple statement: "Take up [your] cross and follow me" (Matthew 16:24). Following Jesus requires more than cleaning up your entertainment habits. It also includes standing up for godly standards, dying to self, and truly committing everything to Him.

I once counseled a mother who was concerned about the amount of MTV her daughter was watching—especially when the mother was at work. I offered some suggestions, but she had tried them all before and they hadn't worked. Her daughter was still watching a lot of MTV.

Finally I said, "MTV is available only on cable. If you really don't want your daughter to watch it, just cancel the cable service!" It seemed like the only solution.

After a few moments of stunned silence, the mother hesitantly muttered, "If we cancel cable, we'll get hardly any channels. My husband and I would miss all the shows *we* enjoy." The tone of her voice told me that she couldn't imagine doing such a "drastic" thing.

"Well," I said, "the choice is yours. How important is your daughter's spiritual well-being?"

This mother was really struggling with the idea that she might have to cut down on her own TV viewing in order to help her daughter at a crucial time. It was a real test to see if she was truly committed to her daughter's growth. I left it up to her to choose whether she was willing to submit her own TV habits to the Lord. If not, how could she ask her daughter to sacrifice MTV for Him?

These choices are hard, but they can be worthwhile. When faced with them, we can honestly measure the levels of our faith and joy. We discover that our willingness to make sacrifices for others is one sign of true spiritual health. We also discover that our choices in entertainment provide clues about our own spiritual condition. Understanding these clues will be crucial to dealing with music and media in the home.

Chapter 10

THE WINDOW
TO A
CHILD'S SOUL

●

*"A mirror reflects a man's face, but
what he is really like is shown by the kind of
friends he chooses." (Proverbs 27:19,* TLB)

Almost every day our office receives letters and
phone calls asking for a list of all the "bad rock groups"
or the "Satanic rock bands." Without a proper understanding of young people and their music, such facts can
become clubs with which adults try to beat their children
into submission. It is not our desire to provide weapons
or ammunition that will add to an already tense situation. We would rather provide effective tools for enhancing communication with your children.

The complex problem of contemporary music in
today's Christian family has no simple, one-step solutions. Today's music involves so much more than just
Satanism. Theories about demon beats and backmasking
are speculative at best. They may be fascinating, but few
people are really motivated to sincere, lasting changes for
Jesus because of such arguments. And trying to force our
children to like what we like is not usually constructive,
either.

Perhaps the most misleading idea is believing that a
direct cause-and-effect relationship exists between music
and a child's behavior. We desperately want to blame

music for all the dramatic and destructive changes in our children.

Some people teach that rock music is the primary reason for teenage drug and alcohol abuse, pregnancies, suicides, and Satan worship. These people conclude that if we could just remove the bad musical influences from young lives, all the problems would disappear as well. Then their children could get on with living wholesome and holy lives. Thus parenting is reduced to a simple formula: remove the music, get the kid saved, and everything will be all right.

Obviously, these people have never been parents! Theirs would be a wonderfully convenient solution, if it only worked. But it is quite simplistic and naive. The theory sounds fine until it is actually applied in a real, live family. Then it splits parents and young people and pushes them to opposite extremes of the music spectrum.

At one end are the adults whose arguments just do not hold up given the variables of peer pressure, education, divorce, the family's spiritual condition, the parent/child relationship, or physical/emotional changes that come from simply growing up. These are all important elements in a child's development that cannot be ignored.

At the other end of the spectrum are the equally naive young people who claim that music is not the problem. In fact, they say music has absolutely no effect on them. This claim is also simplistic and shortsighted. Music may not be the only influence in our children's lives, but it is certainly a powerful one.

As is often the case, the truth lies somewhere between the two extremes. Music may indeed influence our children over time. But it does not work like black magic nor should it be completely ignored.

Before we can move on to the practical "how to's" of dealing with rock music in our homes and churches, we should first consider one more concept that can resolve the conflict and eliminate the misunderstanding between the two extremes. It is the key to success in dealing with today's music.

If properly understood and applied, this concept can bring communication, unity, love, and spiritual health back into our families. The secret lies in understanding that today's music is actually a window into your child's soul.

STRAIGHT FOR THE HEART

Today's teenagers relate to their music in very personal ways. Music isn't hypnotizing our children into thinking and behaving in ways that go against their wills. It is not making mindless zombies out of them. Rather, they are embracing the music because someone is saying something with which they can identify.

This sense of identification is usually a gradual, growing process. It is not true of every teenager, but the pattern is very reliable. Preteens and junior-high students tend to gravitate to whatever is popular at the moment. They like the songs their friends like, which is usually the music getting the most radio airplay on the top forty stations.

As teens grow older, they generally have more money to spend on tapes and CDs. They are still greatly influenced by their peers, but they tend to relate to a more specific crowd at school. They choose music that relates to their feelings and their friends. They embrace artists that speak to their personal issues and circumstances. They focus on music that makes them think, *"Yeah, these people know exactly how I feel."*

Young people feel validated when they sense that someone finally understands what they're going through and accepts them just as they are. They crave this person's acceptance, guidance, and promise of escape. They identify with the songs, the group, and almost everything else that goes with the package.

It is important to realize that music affects most teenagers in this way. Some parents believe that music is only entertainment and has no real impact on children's lives other than casual pleasure. Other parents panic and react with urgent hostility, afraid their children will engage in deadly behaviors overnight as a result of listening to one song or album. Neither of these reactions will help children find the answers they need.

Adolescents struggle with feelings of anger, rebellion, sexuality, powerlessness, frustration, lack of self-worth, and depression. If they do not get solid, spiritual help for these struggles at home, they will eventually find answers from their friends, the streets, the media, and especially their music. As young people identify with the feelings of the music, it becomes easy for them to also accept the solutions that the singer offers.

Over time, the music reinforces feelings until they become attitudes. Those attitudes may then develop into values. And a person's values determine his or her choices and behavior. So music has the potential to reinforce values and attitudes in ways that can lead to all sorts of experimental, even destructive, behaviors. It is likely that these attitudes will tend to erode, spoil, deteriorate, distract, and drain the person's spiritual life. But in the midst of this despairing scenario lies a window of hope.

IN SEARCH OF CLUES

Our hope lies in realizing that we can use music as a clue rather than a club. A young person's music is deeply personal to him, so it is almost impossible to condemn the music without making the child feel rejected as well. Our children don't feel that we are attacking some external evil called music. They believe that we are attacking them personally. If we get drawn into this kind of struggle, it will always prove to be a losing battle. Not only will we end up losing the music war, but we may end up losing our children as well.

So how can we use music as a clue? By listening closely to their music, we can discover what our children really feel, what they believe, what they like, and what they need. *But isn't their music providing worldly advice to problems that need spiritual answers?* Of course it is. But if we will take a moment to think this through, we'll get to the source of the real problem: our children's empty hearts.

In chapter six we described a number of music styles that are popular with young people today. Each of these styles provides clues to our children's inner worlds if we will only take a little time to listen and think. Let's now look at how you can use these clues to discover how this music can be a window to your child's soul.

Clues from Dark Music

The somber and pessimistic viewpoint of dark music (new wave, alternative) seems to appeal to the more intellectual, introspective, and passive teen. The music focuses on broken hearts, hurt feelings, and all the things that are wrong with the world. Some of these musical observations are accurate. We are surrounded by war, corruption, foolishness, and selfishness. But the problem with dark music is that it rarely offers an answer. According to these artists, the world is bleak and we have no choice but to sit and stare at the wall, waiting for the end.

Fans of this music tend to think too much and take too little action. They have given up and given in to listless apathy. Their claim that there are no solutions is often a cover-up for poor self-esteem. They feel hopeless, helpless, and inadequate to achieve the kinds of changes they wish they could make. Dark music about an ugly world fits their inner feelings of personal ugliness and worthlessness.

This kind of young person often has too much—too much time, too much money, too much intelligence. We need to offer this type of child goals that will give him a sense of purpose and self-worth. We need to help provide him with a deeper realization of his true value in the sight of Jesus. He needs to experience a sense of meaning through the accomplishment of successful changes in his immediate world.

Clues from Hard Rock

Hard rock displays high energy and colorful imagery. Many young people are led to believe that this music can help them escape the rigors of responsibility and the painful side of life. According to the messages in this music, love is always just around the corner and the party never ends.

Party metal fans are often looking for validation, excitement, and acceptance by their peers because they don't believe it lies within themselves. The answer must be somewhere "out there," in the future. Unsure of themselves, they tend to blame everyone and everything else. They frequently admit to not liking or trusting their present circumstances or environment.

These youth will learn that the party always ends and there are always dues to pay. Perhaps we can guide them to this knowledge sooner, rather than later. We can't always help young people avoid the consequences of their choices. But we can pray that we will be there by their sides when disaster strikes. With wisdom, we can use these teachable, vulnerable moments to show them that their music lied to them. But more than this, we need to affirm that value and security are theirs already—in their family, in their circumstances, and in themselves as unique and special creations of God.

Fans of black metal may also be looking for an escape, but their needs tend to be deeper and darker. This music is based on power and revenge. It offers solutions in black magic which promise the ability to protect oneself, to receive rewards, to accomplish great deeds, and to wreak havoc on enemies. This music appeals to the teen who feels life is out of control or who has been deeply hurt. Sometimes it reflects a cry of anger against a Christian religion that is strangling the would-be sorcerer.

Adults need to look beyond the music to the potentially traumatic events in the lives of these listeners. *What has caused so much fear and rage in their souls? Perhaps death, divorce, abuse, or suicide?* God understands this kind of severe pain. He felt it when His Son died. He also knows how to forgive and help a person begin again.

The crudeness and violence of hardcore might be repulsive to an adult, but it can be very reassuring to an angry adolescent who feels that his world is out of control. Many fans feel inadequate, frustrated, and angry. Perhaps they have good reason to feel the way they do. They may be dealing with an alcoholic parent, a lack of communication in the family, a divorce in the home, or some other unavoidable situation. Such experiences may lead a teen to believe that he must remain in complete control in order to protect himself from painful personal feelings.

Parents and youth leaders can teach these young people that God is in charge and provides order to life, even when life does not seem kind or fair. Even when people fail us, God listens and cares. He is always bigger than our fears, our defeats, and our pain. Teens also need flesh-and-blood models of godly character—people who are both strong decision makers and compassionate listeners. These young fans can then see that God is not an enemy, nor is He an impotent wimp standing by idly while people suffer. If they will make room for Him, He will provide positive action in their lives.

Clues from Rap Music

Rap music reflects much of the same attitude as hardcore. Macho posturing and street-corner bravado are very appealing to young teens, especially boys. Although many protest that they just like the beat, the pulsing lyrics of rap are driving home some strong and damaging messages about self-centered survival and quick-fix sex. While many rappers proudly say no to hard drugs, they still tend to glorify violence, gangs, crime, and life on the streets. Rap can feed the ego of insecure young teens who are in a hurry to be in complete control of their lives.

Parents and youth workers need to be willing to point out the errors in these philosophies promoting sex and violence. Young people need to be reminded that God created women for far greater potential and blessing than to be treated like prostitutes or sexual utensils. The arrogant boasting of many rappers is a poor, self-centered substitute for genuine self-esteem.

God has much better ways to help young people deal with insecurity and poor self-image. His grace and love are the solutions to a faltering heart. His plans for lasting, fulfilling relationships far exceed hit-and-run, instant, sexual gratification. His peace is the answer to gang conflict and rebellion against authority. If we can communicate these positive alternatives in a loving way, intelligent young people won't be fooled by the empty promises of rap music.

Clues from Pop/Dance Music

The sexuality of the pop/dance music of Madonna, Paula Abdul, Janet Jackson, and others tends to concern parents. But many young girls identify with this style of music. By doing so, they may be telling us that they fear they'll never be attractive or loved on their own merits. They may feel a need to act and look like the women in the movies and music videos in order to get the attention they crave.

If a girl's father doesn't treat her as if she is special, she's more likely to believe the musical myths of a song like George Michael's "Father Figure." She will cling to the promise that some guy will come along with just the right words to make her feel good about herself. It's surprising to find out how many attractive young ladies feel inadequate, ugly, and unloved.

God is the true Father figure who loves our daughters just the way they are. But they may need our help to realize what a special treasure they are in His sight. They need regular assurance of His perfect plan for their lives and of their parents' commitment of time, interest, and genuine caring—not just words. "Do not merely listen to the word, and so deceive yourselves. Do what it says" (James 1:22).

Are you beginning to see how your child's music can be a window to his soul? Young people consider their music to be an answer to some very real concerns. It addresses many of their personal and emotional needs. With a few good musical "clues," parents can begin to identify those needs. With prayer and wisdom, we can begin to provide solid, spiritual alternatives to the musical myths our children hear.

Parents, you must be prepared to be part of the answer yourselves. This healing process requires more than just saying the right words. You need to put aside your own biases and anger. You must begin to minister as Jesus would minister. It's really not so hard to do when you don't have to put so much energy into wrestling the music monster. You have more freedom to listen and ask tender questions.

Keep in mind that your child's reaction will depend on your history of communication with him or her. Children might be defensive at first if they feel you are prying. Show a sincere interest, tempered with grace and mercy. Remember, you are asking them to reveal their innermost secrets, some of which they may never have tried to express before.

You can start this sensitive process by asking questions like these:

♪ What are some of your favorite songs?

♪ Why does that song mean so much to you?

♪ Do you ever wonder whether you are going to grow up and survive?

♪ What are your views on sex and love? Has your music helped shape your views?

♪ Are you sometimes angry and frustrated with this family?

These are dangerous questions to ask if we don't want to hear the truth. *Do we have a hard time admitting mistakes? Are we afraid of our own inadequacies as parents? Do we really have faith that God can handle the situation? Do we feel comfortable being vulnerable, open, honest, humble, and emotional with our children?* Even if this experience is painful, it is necessary if we are going to truly communicate with our children. If we are going to find out where they hurt, we need to find out what goes on inside them.

120

Today's music speaks to our children. It mirrors their souls. If we want to know the hearts of our children, we must listen to their music and discuss it with them.

ROADBLOCKS TO PROGRESS

After years of counseling, speaking, and raising my own children, I've realized that there are a number of roadblocks that parents encounter when trying to communicate spiritual values to their children. Encouraging your child to open up to you is usually easier said than done. Here are some common problems you may experience.

The Problem Child

A pastor at one of my seminars told me, "Our family used to have a problem with rock music, but we don't anymore. He moved out." I could hardly believe what I was hearing. This man was the pastor of a major conservative, evangelical church admitting that he had been defeated by the issue of rock music! He struggled with the music in his home so fiercely for so long that he finally made the crucial mistake of seeing his son as the problem—and even as an enemy.

Let's face it, parents. Our children will *have* problems as they grow up. They will certainly *cause* problems as they grow up. But we make a grave mistake if we start believing that they *are* the problem.

The Bible tells us that, "Children are a gift of the Lord; the fruit of the womb is a reward. Like arrows in the hand of a warrior, so are the children of one's youth. How blessed is the man whose quiver is full of them" (Psalm 127:3-5, *NASB*). Our children are a blessing, they are often a challenge, and they are certainly an experience. But they are never the problem.

Wrong attitudes sneak up on some parents. As time goes by, certain things do not turn out as expected. Our children may disappoint us. They may come to be perceived as an inconvenience and a financial hardship. As a result of these feelings, parents may develop unrealistic expectations or resentment.

We recognize this trend when it occurs in other families around us, but it is difficult to detect in our own lives. We need to be vigilant in our prayers, asking the Lord to show us when we get off course. We must desire to imitate God's love and enthusiasm for our children, to see them as He does.

Facing Failure

Another difficult aspect of raising children is watching them fail. Our instinct is to protect them from any kind of failure. If they fail frequently, we may grow to resent them or try to correct the situation by tightening our control. We may be especially sensitive to potential failures in spiritual areas. We tend to keep on telling them the right thing to do. If they don't respond immediately, we tell them again.

After awhile, of course, this becomes badgering. We are clearly warned not to provoke children (Ephesians 6:4; Colossians 3:21). If we do, they tend to become more angry, discouraged, rebellious, and resentful with each lecture. If a parent never lets up and the child's personal resentment grows, it may soon spread to include religion, God, and everything else the parent stands for.

This approach only pushes our children farther and farther away from us—and from God. We become so consumed with pointing out the evil in rock music that we neglect to show our children we love them. We forget that our goal is to bring them closer to Jesus. Anger has a way of crowding God out of the picture. If a child's immediate concern is to avoid our anger, it is unlikely he will be motivated to seek God.

Angry badgering doesn't always result in a child's visible rebellion. But the lack of an outward struggle doesn't guarantee that there is no inner struggle. This is illustrated by the story of the 3-year-old girl who found it very hard to be good in church. She stood up on the pew continually. She waved to Grandma. She blew her nose loudly during the pastor's prayer. She talked to others within earshot. Each time her mother sat her down, she would pop up again. Finally, Mother grabbed her by the muscle between the neck and shoulder (which I believe God put there for situations like this) and forced her to stay seated. Though unable to move, the little girl looked up defiantly and said, "I might be sitting down on the outside, but I'm standing up on the inside."

This attitude is typical of many churched children today. It doesn't seem possible, but our ministry is finding that the vast majority of children raised by Christian parents do not end up living for Jesus as adults. Some studies suggest this number is as high as seventy to eighty percent.

Another remarkable statistic is the number of secular rock artists whose parents were pastors or churchgoers. Parents are usually shocked to see a child drift away from home, leaving his or her Christianity on the doorstep. The parents want to blame the secular college, their child's new friends, drugs, alcohol, or rock music.

How is the situation at your home, Christian parent? How do you express your faith? Do you communicate in a way that reflects your faith and joy in Christ? Or do you communicate fear, anger, hysteria, a critical spirit, and a desperation to be in control? *Do you give your children answers to their deep personal and spiritual questions, or do you leave that job to the church?* Are you willing to accept some responsibility for your child's future? Are you doing all you can for Jesus, or only what you have to? Is rock music really the reason your child is failing to follow Christ? *Are you teaching your children how to think and find spiritual answers for themselves, or do you only tell them what to think?*

Quick Solutions

Some parents are filled with a false sense of accomplishment and don't even notice their children slipping away. Perhaps they have succeeded in banning rock music from their home, destroying albums and posters, and making restrictive rules about friends, music purchases, and concerts. But they don't realize that removing the rock music only removes the symptoms. It does not provide any deep and lasting solutions.

Even worse, the parent misses out on helping the child solve his root spiritual problems. For instance, removing the distasteful tapes of some obnoxious hard-rock group will not remove the anger and frustration that attracted the child to that group in the first place. In fact, it will probably just make the problem worse! If a parent vetoes all such music in the home, the child will usually seek it out in other settings (almost always in places less spiritual and less healthy). Not only that, but the action closes the door to any communication the parent may have had with the child.

With the symptoms of trouble out of sight, the parent probably stops looking for problems and thinks, *"I guess I showed him who's boss."* That settles that. The parent may have won that battle, but will ultimately lose the war for the child's soul.

The potential roadblocks of problem children, failure, and quick solutions show why it is so important to see your child's music as a window to his soul and a clue to his spiritual needs. It helps you keep your real goals in perspective. Our children are not our problem or our enemy. Neither is the music. We are not wrestling against flesh and blood, so why do we think the solutions to our problems lie in banning posters and tapes? They are only the material (flesh) aspects of the problem.

The problem is not the music, but rather the effect the music has on our faith in Jesus and the joy of our salvation. The struggle here is for our children's souls. Our energies in this struggle should not be so much to draw our children *away* from the music as to draw them *toward* Christ.

THE RIGHT ROAD

Caring parents should be eager to become a child's spiritual role models and help him find genuine answers to his struggles. By demonstrating honest concern and using the clues that his music provides, we can draw him out and show him that Christ provides real answers to his hurts and doubts.

We need to be sure we let God have His way in our own lives first. We need to step aside and let the Holy Spirit do His job. He will convict them of any sin they may have committed, but in His timing—not ours! Jesus loves your children just the way they are, but too much to leave them that way. Do we reflect His character enough to communicate the same attitude? What do we really reflect about Christ and Christianity when we discuss music with our children?

Our goal as parents goes far beyond simply lecturing about the evils of the world or rock music. We cannot expect our children to understand about faith and joy if we do not demonstrate these qualities ourselves. And of course, modeling these things for our children will require an investment of time.

We must love our children more than we hate rock music. We must put our feelings aside so we can focus on spiritual things. We must develop patience to keep trying when we don't succeed at first, humility to allow the Holy Spirit to accomplish the real spiritual work, and vulnerability to share what Jesus means to us. We must practice good listening skills to discover what's really on our children's hearts, and complete dependence on Christ and Him alone. This kind of parenting will be the most challenging and fulfilling task you can undertake on this earth. ♩

Chapter 11

"WHAT SHOULD I DO IF MY CHILD LISTENS TO ROCK MUSIC?"

"Do not exasperate your children;
instead, bring them up in the training and
instruction of the Lord." (Ephesians 6:4)

It may seem as though we've taken a long time to get to this chapter and to the question posed in its title. Perhaps you bought this book for the sole purpose of finding out what to do if your child listens to rock music. The question is certainly the one I hear most often as I talk to parents and adults who work with young people.

Yet I hope you understand by now that this is not a simple problem to tackle. I felt it was important to lay the groundwork and let you know how I came to my conclusions. Like you, I have agonized over this issue—not only as a speaker, but also as a parent. These ideas are much more than theories to me. My staff and I have experimented, prayed, and searched diligently for the best biblical answers.

It is with confidence that we say the answers lie in treating your children as gifts from God whom you want to see conformed to the character of Christ. The desire to build positive communication within the family is the key. With these insights, we can begin to realistically respond to the problem of rock music with some hope of success. So now, at last, let's look at a practical, step-by-step approach for dealing with rock music in the home.

1. START ON YOUR KNEES

So often when I say the first and best thing to do is to pray, I get a knowing look of smugness. I can tell that everyone is thinking, *Yes, of course, but what should I really do?*

What should we really do? Pray! We can't do anything more powerful or more effective than that. (See James 5:16.) We must not treat prayer as a spiritual cliché. God knows our concerns! He cares! He desires to hear from us. If Christian parents spent 30 minutes each day in fervent prayer for their children, do you believe their children would be different? If so, why aren't more of us doing it?

Every Christian intends to pray more than he actually does. *Do you pray for your children every single day?* Many parents pray with their children as they recite little rehearsed prayers at bedtime. But how often do you pray for them as they sleep or as you watch them go off to school? *Do you regularly pray for their souls, for their futures, for their future spouses, and for their spiritual maturity?*

I must confess that occasionally I start slipping in this important responsibility. I let the pressure of urgent deadlines force me into hurried prayers. But usually, before long, I am prompted by the Holy Spirit to remember how my mother prayed faithfully for me. She taught me that we may pray for our children for many years without seeing results, yet we must keep praying in obedience to the will of God.

When you're ready to deal with the issue of rock music, here are some prayer concerns you might want to consider:

♪   Pray for wisdom and a loving attitude.

♪   Pray for the patience to treat your children as gifts from your heavenly Father and to remember that they are *not* the problem.

♪   Pray that you'll be able to control your emotions during your discussions.

♪   Pray that you'll be able to give priority to the things God wants to teach them, giving the Holy Spirit room to do His work.

♪   Pray that your children will be open to these discussions.

♪   Pray that you and your children will be able to listen to and trust one another.

♪   Pray that you can effectively let them know that you care and understand.

♪   Pray for enhanced communications. The Lord promises to give us the right words to speak when we get into difficult situations (Matthew 10:19). Pray for the right words, believing God will fulfill His promise.

2.   SET ENTERTAINMENT GUIDELINES FOR YOUR FAMILY

Sit down with your spouse and discuss your current and future entertainment guidelines. Be as honest and realistic as possible. Where do you stand? How much are you willing to tolerate? How much media do you want in your home? What kinds? What about tapes, CDs, radio, videos, TV? Will you allow rock posters on the walls? Is it okay to buy and read rock magazines? Do you want to set a daily limit on the amount of rock music or TV? Do you want restrictions on volume?

Pray about these guidelines and put them down in writing. Begin with what you think would be ideal. List what you are willing to put up with. You may want to discuss your guidelines with your pastor or youth director for additional feedback, especially if you are a single parent. Honestly evaluate whether these guidelines are fair to your children. Do they honestly reflect your faith? Are they biblical? Can you explain why? Make sure you can express your convictions in terms that everyone in the family can understand.

Parents may be tempted to enforce the limits they've set by sneaking into their children's rooms while the kids are at school and tossing out music that doesn't meet the guidelines. This action will not enhance family communications or glorify God. Children need to learn to make spiritual commitments for themselves. They need a model for arriving at spiritual decisions that they can understand and imitate.

Be prepared for a number of discussions. Do not try to accomplish everything in one meeting. You cannot discuss complex biblical issues regarding music, radio, TV, movies, magazines, and other forms of entertainment in one sitting. You will need to address these issues in bite-sized pieces that can be digested and acted on without causing major upheaval in the family structure. Remember, the goal is to draw the family closer to Christ and to each other, not just to lay down the law.

If you decide to eliminate some of the entertainment from your home, decide how to restructure the extra time you create. For instance, if your third grader is watching too many hours of cartoons on TV in the morning and you cut the amount in half, how can you replace those hours with constructive activity? It has to be something that the child considers interesting and meaningful. We cannot take away his TV time and then have him wash the dishes instead. Rather, find an option that will bring the family closer together and help the child understand how to glorify Jesus Christ.

Along with the guidelines, develop a predetermined course of action to help enforce them. How are you going to measure the limits set for TV viewing? How will you monitor music listening in the home? How are you going to respond if the guidelines are violated? How many warnings will your children be given? What if a parent violates the guidelines? Be prepared to explain and justify your responses.

Setting guidelines generally works best when the children are still preschool or in elementary school. Parents of these age groups have a lot of authority and the ability to guide their children in making spiritual decisions. The earlier you determine the parental limits in your home, the better it will be for your family.

3.   MAKE CERTAIN YOUR ACT IS TOGETHER

Have you honestly and biblically evaluated the entertainment areas of your own life? Have you set harder standards for your children than for yourself, or is the example consistent in your home? (You may want to review chapter nine.)

Are both parents in clear agreement about the limits that were set? If you do not present a united front, your children will play one parent against the other to get what they want. But if the guidelines are well written, they will not be subject to the changing moods of a parent or child. Fair enforcement of the rules will be as much of a discipline for you as for your children.

This process is somewhat different for a single parent. If the other spouse is not involved in child rearing, then the active parent must do his or her best to enforce the guidelines alone. In many divorce situations, the other parent is still partly involved through weekend parenting or summer custody. If you still have an amicable relationship, explain your guidelines and convictions. Try to come to an agreement so the child will be treated the same by both parents.

If, however, the other parent is not agreeable, still angry, hurting over the relationship, or a non-Christian, you have a more serious problem than music in your home (though music will often be the symptom of the unrest such a situation creates in your children's lives). If this is your situation, seek counseling for the real issues at hand, and pray that God will bring unity and salvation through these difficult circumstances.

4. EXPLAIN YOUR GUIDELINES TO YOUR CHILDREN

Sit down with your whole family and discuss the limits you have set. Gather around the kitchen table after dinner or on Saturday morning at breakfast. Turn off the TV and shut out any other distractions. Tell your children about your convictions concerning the influences of music and entertainment. Be willing to concede that they might not understand or share your feelings, and be vulnerable enough to confess if you haven't been living up to the proposed standards yourself.

Share your earnest desire to live more consistently for God. Explain to your children that, like Daniel, you have purposed in your heart not to defile yourself with the "diet" the entertainment world offers (Daniel 1). Let them know that in your home, you intend to let your Christian principles and ethics determine which media are acceptable—no matter what other families are doing. State your reasons clearly.

Your children might not agree with all the limits you set, and they are likely to ask a lot of questions. They may see the proposed changes as punishment, rather than a rewarding experience. Be ready to give them biblical reasons for your decisions. Make sure they understand that you are not reacting out of fear or anger.

Be open-minded enough to listen to your children. Some of their complaints may be silly, immature, defiant, or spiritually foolish. But others may be legitimate excuses you never have thought of, personally important to the child because of peer pressure, school requirements, or any number of reasons. Our children often have a simple wisdom that can keep us in balance.

Be prepared to bend a little, compromise, or even change some of the rules. Don't break your family because you're unwilling to bend. Love and respect your children enough to consider what they have to say. As the parents, you have the final word, but this cannot mean your children are to have no say whatsoever. As a family, put a plan together that is biblical, feasible, enforceable, and spiritually healthy.

Strive to give your children a sense of security, rather than a feeling of hysteria or dread. They may test the new guidelines to see if your resolve is serious. But when they understand where the limits are, they will feel more secure. This can be a rewarding, constructive process. It also gives your children an effective model by which to explain their entertainment choices to friends later on.

After everyone has discussed the new guidelines, prepare a written contract for the family. Write down how the family will evaluate and choose music, purchase tapes, watch television, and so forth. Put the result of your discussions in print and give each family member a copy.

For example, my wife and I do not allow our daughters to have secular music that teaches unbiblical philosophies. We allow them to listen to an occasional secular recording that is inoffensive or biblically consistent, and they may buy one if they are willing to spend their own money on it. However, my daughters know I will buy any Christian music they want because I consider it an investment in their future spiritual growth.

133

Our family television viewing is based on the verse, "I will set no worthless thing before my eyes" (Psalm 101:3, *NASB*). We actually have that verse written in calligraphy on a card which sits on our TV. If a program's content is against biblical values, we won't let it come into our home through television. And this guideline doesn't change after the children go to bed. If it is wrong for them, it is also wrong for my wife and me.

Obviously, a discussion of guidelines usually works best in a home setting in which both parents are Christians and the children are young. In such an environment, these discussions can be warm, fun, and enlightening. Parents and children can both grow spiritually. And in the desire to please their parents, young children will often set stricter limits for themselves than what you would demand. They can experience the rewards of properly responding to the freedom and encouragement you give them.

However, many families do not fit the ideal situation. In those homes, some of these steps become a bit more difficult. You may be tempted to resist this discussion altogether with the excuse that you work too hard and need to relax in front of the tube. But it is essential to take these steps if you are truly concerned about the entertainment in your home.

5.   SPEND TIME WITH YOUR TEENS

I once heard a policeman describe the arrest of a young man who was the leader of a group of Satan worshipers in Texas. The whole community was shocked by the arrest because the young man had appeared to be a clean-cut, exemplary citizen. He was getting straight A's in school and was involved in several social clubs, so his secret involvement in Satanism came as a complete surprise—especially to his mother.

The investigators went to his home to search for clues about his Satanic involvement. They had to break down the door to his room because there was a lock on it. Only the young man had the key. The police found rock posters, demonic literature, a locker full of materials to use as an altar to Satan, and even tapes of a psychodrama in which the young man portrayed himself as being possessed by the devil.

His mother later confessed that she had not set foot in his room for more than three years. All his activities had gone unchecked because she had refused to become involved in his life. She thought that she was communicating to her son that she was giving him freedom. But what she really communicated was that she didn't care about him. The son's shocking lifestyle was allowed to become excessive because his mother was out of touch with what he was doing.

I've met parents who are proud of the fact that they don't have the slightest idea what kinds of music their children listen to. They boast that they don't know the difference between White Christmas and White Zombie. Not only are these parents out of touch, they are also giving the impression that they don't love their children.

What if you did something four, six, or even eight hours a day without your spouse expressing an interest in it—even in passing? You might come to believe that he or she doesn't care about you as a person. You might even doubt whether he or she really loves you. After investing valuable hours each day, the person who is supposed to love you doesn't even know what you're doing. Eventually, you would be likely to resent your spouse because of his or her lack of interest.

Now think. *How much interest do you show in the things your child enjoys?* Teenagers today spend two to six hours a day listening to music. Anything that consumes so much of their time must be pretty important to them. Yet some parents don't even have a clue what groups their children like. How sad! The implication is that the parents just don't care.

This attitude makes it easier for young people to justify their alienation from parents. After all, their parents haven't even taken the time to find out what's so important to them. But when parents truly show an interest in the things that interest young people—even rock music— their children will be more likely to expose true feelings, dreams, and desires.

Parents need to become acquainted with the music and TV habits of their children. *Do the kids have a television, a VCR, or a radio in their room? What have they been watching and listening to? Do they watch horror movies or sexual movies when they get with their friends? What kinds of CDs and tapes do they have in their collection? What radio stations do they listen to? Who are their favorite groups?*

After you answer these questions, do some research on any of the groups that are new to you. (Our ministry can help you with this.) Begin building bridges by indicating that you can say something intelligent about your child's music—not just that it's Satanic, awful, or disgusting. Real facts are effective tools in opening up communication with your children. When they see that you honestly know something about their music, they realize that you are truly interested in them and what goes on in their world. It is important to develop a rapport with your child about his music.

Remember, the biggest sacrifice God asks parents to make is the sacrifice of time. Good communication with your teenage children won't take place in a day, a week, or even a month. It can be a long, growing process.

6. WEED OUT UNACCEPTABLE ENTERTAINMENT

After meeting as a family to discuss entertainment guidelines, move the discussion into your child's room to discuss each person's entertainment, one at a time. Survey the child's room in regard to wall decorations, stereos, radios, TVs, VCRs, cassettes and CDs, and so forth. (It is better not to let the child accumulate all of these electronic toys. It's not much of a punishment option to restrict a child to a room equipped like a luxury hotel!)

Once a survey has been made of your child's room, make specific applications to your guidelines. It might be easier to start the discussions on the topic of television. Together, you can decide what programs to watch or not watch. Then discuss when the radio can be listened to, and what videos should be allowed on the VCR in the room. Later discussions can bring up the subject of rock music.

Talk to your child about his faith and joy. Are they everything he wants them to be? *Is he questioning his salvation or the validity of the Bible? Does he wonder if God is real and if He really cares? Does he exhibit the fruit of the Spirit in his life—love, joy, peace, and so forth (Galatians 5:22, 23)? Has he ever struggled with thoughts of suicide? Is he feeling depressed? How does he handle negative feelings? What does his music mean to him? Is it a primary means of escape?*

Remain alert to the possibility that your children may not be genuinely saved. (You may come to that conclusion as you talk with them.) If this is the case, consider being less strict on the rock music issue. Your main concern shouldn't be their listening habits; it should be the condition of their soul. Begin to deal with issues like music, discipline, and school with a focus on how you can help your children come to know Christ.

With your child still in the room with you, examine his tapes and CDs—group by group. *What are the philosophies of these musicians and how do they compare with what Jesus teaches?* Ask if the music encourages him to focus on things above rather than on earthly things (Colossians 3:2).

You might ask a younger child, "Do the singers love Jesus?" If the child is older, you can ask, "Does the music encourage spiritual growth in your life?" If the child answers "No," ask, "Can you afford to be influenced by this group?" If the child answers "Yes," ask, "How is the music helping you grow spiritually?"

Asking these questions shifts the burden of responsibility from your shoulders to his. It is left up to him to make a positive decision. You no longer need to be your child's judge. If his answers satisfy you, thank God for your child's wisdom and maturity. Use this time to draw closer to your child and express the faith you hold together.

These may be difficult questions for your child to answer. He might respond, "I don't know," and shrug a lot. Press for real answers to your questions about his spiritual condition. Be patient and wait for specific answers to your specific questions. Here are some excuses I suggest you don't accept:

♪ *"I don't listen to the words!"*—Just play one of your child's favorite songs and see how easily he remembers the lyrics. He may not realize it, but his subconscious mind is fully aware of what's being sung.

♪ *"It doesn't affect me!"*—How can he be certain? If his faith and joy aren't strong, his entertainment could be a major influence.

♪ *"The musicians are only performing (immoral music) for the fun, money, and/or fame!"*—Who cares why they do it? The point is that their music is being

138

produced and bought. Even if their motives aren't evil, the results on the listener may be!

♪ *"I don't listen to evil (or Satanic) music."*—Have the child define evil. The majority of secular music promotes philosophies that are against biblical values. Doesn't it make more sense to listen to music that ministers, instead of music that is merely inoffensive?

Your children probably won't want to analyze their music. They just want to enjoy it. But push them gently and firmly toward the process of evaluating what they listen to. Help them investigate the possibility that their music contributes to their lack of spiritual growth, their dissatisfaction with the church, their irritation by friends in certain relationships, or other problems they may be facing. Their music may be giving them ideas that are creating or exaggerating these problems.

It isn't wise to start by throwing out your child's entire music collection. But remove offensive groups as you find them, and explain why you are doing so. Start with the worst music first and move to the middle ground. Don't take away undesirable music without offering something to take its place. *Are you willing to substitute better stuff for the rock music you take away?*

I suggest that you offer to replace the most offensive albums with Christian music. In addition to providing entertainment, Christian music is a valuable tool to help a believer focus on life from God's point of view. Used effectively, it can strengthen your child's spiritual life. (More will be said on this subject in the next chapters.)

Before you recoil at the potential expense of exchanging a Christian recording for every offensive tape or CD in your child's collection, think of it as an investment. Investments may be expensive, but they return dividends. I believe you'll see the dividends in your child as he grows in the Lord through the influence and encouragement of Christian music.

Christian music is available in almost every style imaginable. If you don't know what Christian music artists to substitute for your child's groups, go to your local Christian bookstore. Many have listening centers that will allow you to sample a wide variety. Also, feel free to contact our office.

7.   REEVALUATE YOUR GUIDELINES

Parents often discover that discussions with children prove to be quite revealing—even surprising. Adults usually have specific expectations about the child's condition and what needs to be done. But after actually talking and listening to their children, many parents find that the situation is completely different than they expected.

Parents may need to renegotiate the contract, set new limits, or alter the standards according to what they discover. Some parents will find that their children are more deeply involved in secular music than they believed possible. Others will find that their children are much more mature than they had realized. It's amazing how quickly we can get out of touch with our children's lives.

Don't compromise your spiritual and family values, but don't be stubborn either. Be willing to adjust and reset limits that will be most constructive for the child. You don't need to settle these complex issues overnight. Children grow gradually, so don't panic. God is in control. Show that you trust Him, and make it clear that you want to trust your children, too.

Before I had children, I thought I had all the answers. Now I realize some boundaries are open for discussion and others are firm. R-rated movies, immoral television programs, and music opposed to biblical values are not open for discussion. Other decisions are. If I don't learn to bend in nonessentials, I am likely to break any positive relationship I might ever have with my children.

Let me share an example of what I mean. Originally, when we set up guidelines with our daughters, we decided they would include only Christian posters in their bedrooms. One day I noticed my older daughter had a picture on her wall of a cute young man who starred in a television show our family watched regularly. Although he was a clean-cut, nice young man, the picture didn't fit within the guideline we had set.

Should I make her take it down or should I bend my limits? After a healthy discussion, we chose to include moral, clean-cut guys in our revised limits. Did I capitulate and allow my daughter to control me? I don't believe so. I decided to bend to prevent my relationship with my daughter from breaking. The important thing is that we talked it out and kept our relationship open.

The key to goal setting is to put goals into bite-sized chunks—steps that are easily achievable. Give children these kinds of goals. If a child has two hundred albums, he probably isn't going to want to throw them out by tomorrow. Discuss the music, group by group and album by album, until you have a collection that reflects the limitations you've set in the home. Freely admit your mistake if you find that you misjudged a group or if you heard a rumor that turned out to be untrue. Being honest is not the same as being wishy-washy.

The ultimate goal in this entire process should be to strengthen our faith and joy, to open up communication within the family, and to help our kids become strong Christians who reflect the character and love of Christ.

WHAT TO THINK OR HOW TO THINK?

We need to teach our kids that we desire to serve Christ and to be unified as a family. We also want to teach them how to make spiritual decisions for themselves. Parents must let go of the reins little by little, whether they are ready or not. The most difficult thing for a parent to do is watch growth in their children occur slowly.

As we attempt to teach Christian values, a major frustration can be waiting for the child to accept what we say. We know from experience that we are right! We know Jesus Christ is God. We believe the Bible is true—every word. We know there is no other way to salvation than through Jesus. We are saved by grace through His shed blood.

These are the very basics of our belief. And because we know the truth, it is often difficult not to give our children all the answers. In fact, when they resist, we want to force the truth on them. After all, we know we are right. If we don't give them the right answers, they might never find them.

But would you send your child to a school that gave tests with all the answers already filled in? What if your child only had to sign his name on the test to get an "A"? At such a school your child would never learn to think and solve problems on his own.

And yet, this is what happens in many Christian homes, churches, and schools across the country. Parents are filling in all the answers for their children's questions about life, God, and Christianity. The children aren't taught to search the Scriptures and learn for themselves. They aren't trained to think critically and discover right from wrong. They aren't allowed to make decisions for themselves.

Many decisions are being made for young people without discussion or explanation—"Just sign your name." And we are quick to label those who won't "sign" as troublemakers. Maybe your troublemaker is simply expressing frustration at not being allowed to think for himself!

Too often in the church we have taught our kids *what* to think, not *how* to think. Churches are full of young people who recite all the right answers and look like "good Christians" on the outside. We have given them all the answers, told them what to do, and dictated how they should live. But we haven't told them how to discern truth through Scripture, how to serve Christ, or how to make good decisions.

When these children leave home, we might have filled in the answers for issues A, B, and C. But if the world throws something new at them, they have no idea how to respond. Why? We've spent too much time getting them to conform to *our* desires instead of helping them discover *God's!*

A former student of mine had parents who kept her on a tight rein. She was allowed to make very few decisions—even on little things. Outwardly, she looked like the perfect child. She got good grades, had lots of friends, and never got into trouble. But later, as an adult, life became quite different for her. She is married for a third time, has alienated herself from her former school friends and family, and is very antagonistic toward the things of Christ. In fact, she is very vocal in her radical, liberal beliefs.

As I think back to her school years, I remember that she was afraid to express herself. She was never taught to think spiritually on her own. Now that she no longer has the restraint of her parents, she freely expresses the anger and hatred that had been bottled up for years. She sees no purpose for Christianity except as a set of rules to keep people like her in line. Her parents still don't understand that her rebellion just might have something to do with her legalistic upbringing.

Parents, how many times have you seen this same scenario take place at your church or even in your own home? Do you know people who know the truth of the gospel and try to force it down their children's throats? We've already said that seventy percent or more children raised by Christian parents never live for Jesus Christ as adults. We must begin teaching our children how to think instead of merely telling them what to think.

We don't help our children if we just dictate which musical groups to listen to, which albums to buy, and which movies to watch. We need to set guidelines and show them how to make these decisions for themselves. If we are loving and patient as we work with them, they are more likely to desire God and seek His answers for their questions. After all, that's the real goal of dealing with rock music in our children's lives. ♪

Chapter 12

THE PURPOSE OF MUSIC

●

*"Be filled with the Spirit. Speak to
one another with psalms, hymns and
spiritual songs. Sing and make music in your
heart to the Lord." (Ephesians 5:18, 19)*

Many moons ago, before the white man came to America, a brave Indian warrior grew in such wisdom and strength that he became chief of a mighty tribe. The son of this chief was a strong and handsome boy, yet he did not evidence all the strengths of his father. He did not always shoot his arrows straight and true. He was not always successful in the hunt. He could not always run as fast or wrestle as skillfully as the other boys.

Everyone in the Indian nation admired their wise chief and showered great praise on him for his wise leadership. But no one admired him more than his young son. With all of his heart he desired to be like his father. But he fell short in so many ways. How could he ever fill his father's moccasins and become a great chief himself? Many evenings he would crawl out on the great rock that overlooked the lake, and ponder his problems until the moon set behind the mountains. Would he ever become wise and strong like his father, or was he destined to bring shame on his family?

One quiet afternoon when the young brave could bear it no longer, he dared to approach his father. Sitting together in their tepee, the young man poured out his ambitions and his fears to his father. His father listened patiently and did not speak for a long time.

Finally, his father looked at him with understanding eyes and replied: "My son, I remember the days of my youth. I struggled just as you do. It was as though there were two dogs within me. One was a good dog, and for a while it seemed to triumph as I would exult in great deeds. I felt as though I would always accomplish mighty exploits. But then a bad dog would come along and fight with the good dog and pull him down. For a while the bad dog would triumph and I would fail at everything. Constantly they fought back and forth in my young life."

The young brave's eyes lit up with recognition as his father spoke: "Yes, Father, I feel the two dogs fighting within me! Some days the good dog seems to be winning the battle. Other days the bad dog seems to have driven the good dog out of me completely. But, Father, how can I be sure the good dog will win in my life?"

The father looked at his son with great compassion and said, "Son, the answer is very simple. The dog who wins is the one you feed the most."

This story has spiritual parallels. Each Christian has two warring factions inside: an "old man" and a "new man," like the "bad dog" and "good dog." The legend admonishes us to starve the bad dog and feed the good dog. Whether the old man or the new man wins out in our lives depends entirely on which one we feed.

We eat food to provide nourishment for our bodies. We also need to feed our minds, our hearts, and our spirits. Scripture tells us that we are to feed the spiritual nature in us with the milk and meat of the Word of God (1 Peter 2:2; 1 Corinthians 3:2; Hebrews 5:12-14).

Which dog is winning in your life? Many of us attend church only one or two hours a week, yet spend hours upon hours feeding ourselves with entertainment of the world. When the average teenager listens to rock music two to six hours a day, that's a lot of musical food for the bad dog. We must do more than shut off the TV, silence the rock music, and stop feeding the bad dog. We must also feed the good dog by focusing on what is good, pure, and undefiled (Philippians 4:8). But how can we do this? I know of no better tool to help us fulfill this command than Christian music.

A LOOK AT YOUR MUSIC DIET

We consume a great deal of media "food." We fill our minds with input from TV, movies, and music. In order to understand what we are consuming, let's break down today's music into four basic food groups.

Evil

Healthy people do not knowingly drink poison or consume the moldy, green stuff that grows in the back of their refrigerators. It's poison! It will make us deathly ill! And it probably won't taste too good, either! We avoid it because we've learned that it is not good for us.

Mature Christians will also avoid the obviously evil ideas presented in the media, especially in music. We have no desire to partake of the overt Satanism or graphic pornography that is presented in some of today's music. Even the young Christians will usually avoid something as obviously Satanic as bands like Danzig or Deicide. And many of them will admit that the sex is too blatant on a 2 Live Crew album and the cursing and violence are too graphic on most gangsta rap albums. Some of this stuff obviously looks, tastes, and feels like poison to our spirits. Wise "diners" avoid it like the plague.

But an amazing number of Christians consume huge quantities of the world's garbage without giving it a second thought! The world sugarcoats a lot of poisonous ideas in their music, and a spoonful of sugar seems to help the garbage go down. Just because something tastes good doesn't mean it's good for you.

This is why I keep coming back to Colossians 2:8. If we are going to truly understand what's good for our spiritual health, we need regular reminders that philosophies that contradict and undermine Jesus' teachings will hurt our faith and joy. We may not feel the effects of such spiritual food poisoning at first. But gradually we will notice that we are losing the stamina to fight our great spiritual battles. Eventually, we become too weak to fight temptation. We become so drained of our passion, energy, and fervor for God, that we no longer find time to read the Bible, share the gospel, or go to church. If we're going to stay spiritually fit, we have to avoid the obviously evil poisons of this world.

Empty

A lot of young people agree with us about music that is obviously evil. However, they frequently ask us about "neutral" music. *What about music that isn't overtly evil? Is it okay for Christians to listen to secular music as long as it's not really bad?*

Spiritually speaking, this kind of music is not neutral—it's empty. I like to call it "Twinkie" music. It won't poison your system, but it won't add nutritional value either. An occasional Twinkie with your lunch is not going to send you to the hospital. But if you ate nothing but Twinkies for every meal, you'd soon get sick of Twinkies. And if you persisted with this diet, you might die of malnutrition eventually. A Twinkie is largely sugar and air. It contains nothing to keep you healthy.

What if Christians fed on musical Twinkies like Green Jelly, Crash Test Dummies ("Mmm, mmm, mmm"), or Weird Al Yankovic ("Eat It!") day in and day out? They would probably become spiritual airheads. Musically speaking, many Christians are feasting on Twinkies. All that sugar and air is leaving them with no substance to their faith or their walk with Christ because they are giving themselves nothing to feed on. Empty music is not an active assault on our spiritual health, but rather a passive death that comes from neglect and lack of nourishment.

Positive

Many songs in the secular market are actually positive. They are moral and uplifting, and they show concern for others. These songs often agree with scriptural principles—love others, feed the poor, shelter the homeless, take responsibility for your choices—without directly referring to Jesus or the Scriptures.

Artists like Mariah Carey and Boyz II Men usually offer a positive, moral picture of love and devotion, with a spiritual flavor. Soul Asylum used the song "Runaway Train" effectively to reach out to runaways and bring them home. Many artists contribute music to positive projects like Habitat for Humanity, Mothers Against Drunk Driving, Farm Aid, and of course, to raise funds for AIDS research. Although it's getting harder to find every day, there are still some songs out there about courage, humility, loyalty, and doing the right thing no matter what it costs.

These songs are the green vegetables in our musical diet—they often provide food for thought. They are good for us, but they may not go down easily. Even Christians need to be reminded occasionally about the struggles going on in the world around us. But we cannot make a complete, balanced meal solely out of green vegetables. They simply do not provide all the nutrients we need. Much of this music asks intriguing and important questions, but does not usually provide the ultimate answer—Jesus. We cannot have a healthy diet until we are feeding on the meat of the gospel—the life, death, and resurrection of Jesus Christ.

Christian

The most neglected musical food group is Christian music, yet it is the most nutritious for our spiritual health! Christian music reflects the teachings of Christ in a way that will strengthen our faith and joy. It is simply Scripture or scriptural principles set to a tune.

The Bible does not define Christian music any more specifically than this. But the Bible *does* explain many ways Christian music can influence our walk with Jesus, strengthen our faith and joy, and keep us spiritually fit.

SCRIPTURAL MUSIC

The clearest passages on music in the New Testament are the parallel passages of Ephesians 5:19 and Colossians 3:16. These verses command believers to sing psalms, hymns, and spiritual songs, singing and making melody in our hearts to the Lord. When the Bible says the same thing twice, we should be aware that it is an important principle of God's Word and not something we should take lightly.

The root of the word for psalms *(psalmos)* means "twitching" in the Greek, as in the twitching of fingers playing an instrument like the harp or lyre. Many of the songs in the Book of Psalms were composed as David expressed God's promises and principles back to Him while playing on his harp. The psalms reflect David's life—his heartaches, questions, and triumphs—as God taught him lesson after lesson about serving Him. They are personal reflections of a heart that belongs to God.

"Hymns" (*humnos* in the Greek) primarily refers to the "hillels," psalms of praise for temple worship. (See Psalms 113–118.) In contrast to most of the other psalms, which are about life with God, hymns are direct praise to God. They describe His attributes, character, and goodness. (A simple way to remember this definition is that "hymns" are about "Him.") Not only are we commanded to reflect on God's impact on our lives, we are also called to praise Him for His many wonderful attributes. We need to be thankful for what He has given us and done for us, and we ought to praise Him for who He is!

Finally, there are spiritual songs. The "song" (*ode* in the Greek) is a spiritual theme set to ordinary tunes of the world. The words in the original language reflect nothing more than this. So while hymns reflect the nature of God and psalms focus on the inner life of the believer, spiritual songs have more of a public emphasis. This could mean that spiritual songs reflect more of the Christian's life in the world at large or spiritual themes aimed at the world—or both.

The distinctions between psalms, hymns, and spiritual songs are crucial to our understanding of a biblical perspective on music. Some people suggest that Christian music is only for praise and worship in a church service, but the Bible indicates that Christian music is that and much more. It is also for personal meditation and encouragement in our hearts as we reflect on Him. (It's a wonderful way to memorize Scripture and learn about the principles in the Word of God.) It is for encouragement and discipleship of others as we share how God has affected our lives. And it can be evangelistic as it reaches out to a hopeless and unsaved world.

If God wanted us to sing Christian music only in church, He would have said so, but He didn't. He commands us to sing psalms, hymns, and spiritual songs in our hearts. The implication is that we should be doing it continually, no matter where we are. I fully believe that if we aren't singing a psalm, hymn, or a spiritual song from our heart to the Lord, we are being disobedient. Period.

These biblical passages reveal how important Christian music should be in the lives of every Christian. Surveys reveal that less than ten percent of the church population listens to Christian music outside the church worship service setting. Why is the percentage so low? It certainly doesn't reflect God's priorities in Scripture. In fact, the longest book in the Bible (Psalms) is a songbook.

We know that godly music was vital to the life of the Old Testament believer. After God delivered the Israelites from the Egyptians, through the crossing of the Red Sea, the first thing they did was to sing a song of praise to the Lord. They ultimately gave thanks, prayed, and built an altar, but the first thing they did was to sing (Exodus 15).

James emphasizes the same principle in the New Testament: "Is anyone cheerful? Let him sing praises" (James 5:13, *NASB*). *What makes you cheerful? What do you do when you're happy? Do you sing praises to God for the goodness He has bestowed on you?*

Through the ages, music has proven to be an excellent tool to help people set their minds and hearts on God. When we sing psalms, hymns, and spiritual songs, we had better understand who God is and why we worship Him. Focusing on the Lord through singing in our hearts also encourages peace and happiness. When we're at peace with God, we'll be spiritually happy. When we're happy, we'll want to sing praises to Him. Are you beginning to get the point? Christian music helps us stay focused on God, which strengthens our faith and joy and maintains a continuous cycle of peace with Christ.

Some people ask, "Aren't we talking about brain-washing here?" Well, as a matter of fact, we are! If you break the word down, it comes out something to the effect of:

brain wash = wash brain = clean brain!

If you wash your brain with propaganda, then brain-washing is harmful. But if you wash your brain with truth, it's the right thing to do. *What are you washing your brain with?*

FIGHTING MUSIC

The Old Testament also shows us that God's music is a great influence during our spiritual conflicts. Throughout the Old Testament, music is associated with victory. Songs of praise accompanied the triumphs of godly people like Deborah (Judges 5), Moses (Numbers 21:16-18), David (1 Chronicles 15:16-28), Nehemiah (Nehemiah 12:27-31, 38-43), and others. And on occasion as the tribes of Israel were going up against their enemies, God's instructions were to put the choir and musical instruments in front of the army.

Today when we read the Old Testament, we may not relate very well to the Israelites. We may think they were too weird, too ancient, or too holy for us. But God's people then were not unlike God's people now. They weren't anxious to face a vicious enemy armed only with robes and choir books. Their enemies had swords, spears, and chariots with spikes on the wheels. Was God trying to make a pincushion out of them?

The situation would be equivalent to the President coming on the airwaves today with an emergency broad-cast: "Our enemies are assembled off the west coast with nuclear missiles prepared to blow up every town, city, and shopping mall in America. But we're ready for them. Our defense will be to assemble every church choir on the beach to sing at the missiles."

Wouldn't this plan sound preposterous? Yet that's exactly what happened as the people of Judah went up against the Moabites and Ammonites under the leadership of King Jehoshaphat. And when they obeyed God and sang at their enemies, they didn't have to lift a sword (or even a finger) in their defense. Instead, the enemy became confused and began to destroy one another (2 Chronicles 20:20-30).

Do you struggle with fear, doubt, and worry? Do certain situations in your life seem impossible to overcome? Don't give up. Sing! When we sing to God, it helps us focus on Him rather than on our problems.

So how does this apply to contemporary life? I believe the church misses out on many opportunities for miracles because we do not have the faith to sing out in the face of our enemies and our problems.

PRAYING MUSIC

Another way Christian music can help us stay spiritually healthy is by helping us with prayer. We are commanded to "pray without ceasing" (1 Thessalonians 5:17). Many Christians assume that this is impossible because we couldn't function if we had to spend every moment on our knees with our eyes closed. But would God give us a command we were incapable of obeying? Obviously not. So perhaps our concept of prayer needs to be adjusted.

I believe the kind of prayer expected of us is the continual conforming of our thoughts to God's thoughts—seeing life from His perspective. Where do we find His thoughts? In His Word, of course. And Christian music is simply Scripture and scriptural principles set to a tune. If we add tunes to God's words and sing them continually, we will eventually discover our thoughts conforming to His. In other words, we can pray without ceasing.

I'm not suggesting that singing should replace your current prayer life. I'm not saying that Christian music will make you spiritual. You must be committed to Jesus Christ in the first place. Unless the music flows naturally from a committed heart, you can sing Christian music until you are blue in the face and it won't do a thing. What I am saying is that Christian music is a wonderful addition to an existing relationship with Christ.

STRAWBERRY JAM

Let me share one more reason why I believe Christian music is so important to spiritual health. When I was a little boy, I couldn't swallow my vitamin pills, which was a major concern in my family. My father was a pill coater by trade, which meant it was his job to put the thin candylike covering on vitamins. We had vitamins in abundance at our house, but it was almost impossible for me to swallow any of them. My mother tried everything to get me to swallow them. I even tried chewing them—once. Have you ever bitten into a vitamin? I thought I was going to die.

My mother finally came up with an idea. She smashed the pill into tiny pieces and covered it with strawberry jam. It didn't go down easily, but I was finally able to swallow my medicine.

Christian music can serve much the same purpose as my mother's strawberry jam. God wants us to be spiritually healthy. To accomplish this, we must learn to swallow certain kinds of spiritual pills that are basic to living a successful Christian life. Oh, you can swallow them without having a song in your heart, but they don't go down as easily as they do when coated with a little musical jam. God's pills are identified in the context of His instructions to sing songs, hymns, and spiritual songs (Ephesians 5:19), so I believe there is an intentional connection.

Pill #1

First, we are to give thanks in all things (Ephesians 5:20). Did you ever try to give thanks in all things? If so, you know it's a hard pill to swallow. But it will go down easier if you coat it with the jam of making melody in your heart to the Lord. If you let Scripture "sing" in your heart when a difficult situation comes along, you'll be more inclined to say "thanks" instead of asking "why."

Do you know people who are bitter, angry, and critical? You can assume that they are also unthankful. More than likely, at some time in their lives they needed to take God at His word and give thanks by faith, but didn't. Problems often start by refusing to thank God for a situation we don't understand.

God isn't cruel. He wants us to be happy. But the only way to do that is by letting Him have control of our lives and thanking Him for *all* things—whether or not we understand His plan. It's hard to do, but it becomes easier if we coat our thanksgiving in the strawberry jam of singing praise to the Lord.

Pill #2

In addition to being thankful to God, we are also to be submissive to one another (Ephesians 5:21). We are to count others' rights as more important than our own. Sometimes this is another bitter pill to swallow.

One specific example of how to incorporate this principle is given in verse twenty-two, where wives are commanded to be submissive to their husbands as unto the Lord. Wives are to treat their husbands with the same respect they would give to Jesus. But since the general principle in verse twenty-one commands all of us (women and men) to be submissive to one another, everyone should treat every other person in the body of Christ with the same respect due to Jesus.

Would you treat a friend with more respect if he or she were Jesus? You bet you would. It's not easy, but believe me, it is a lot easier to be submissive when your heart is coated with the strawberry jam of Christian music.

Pill #3

Unconditional love is a third pill. "Husbands, love your wives, just as Christ loved the church and gave himself up for her" (Ephesians 5:25). The world says love is getting all you can. The Bible describes love as giving: "For God so loved the world that he gave..." (John 3:16). Following God's example of love requires lots of giving, which is exactly the opposite of what the world teaches.

Do you love your husband or wife so much you are willing to give sacrificially to meet the other's needs? Can you ignore the world's obsession with getting and instead be obsessed with giving? Again, it's not easy, but it becomes easier when you are singing a spiritual song in your heart to the Lord. If McDonald's and other advertisers can get you to remember their messages by adding tunes to them, Christians should more easily remember God's important messages by adding a melody to His Word.

Pill #4

Here's a bitter pill for lots of people: obedience. Ephesians 6:1 reads, "Children, obey your parents." Young people often reply, *"But you don't know my parents!"* I don't have to. God does, and He says to obey them in all things.

Teenagers say, "My parents don't understand me." That may be true, but how hard do they try to understand their parents? Young people don't always stop to think about the sacrifices parents make to raise a family. Many kids think only about what *they* want.

A few years ago I conducted a youth seminar on parent/child relationships entitled "How to Wrap Your Parents around Your Finger." My secret was for young people to find out their parents' needs and then to meet those needs (which, by the way, is the biblical definition of love). It's not always easy for children to obey their parents, but listening to Christian music can make it easier.

Parents, do you want your children to be loving, respectful, and obedient to you? Then provide them with Christian music. Teach them to sing in their hearts to the Lord. Good Christian music is available for all ages, so start when they're young. (You'll like it, too. I love my daughters' music, and we enjoy listening to it together.) If you really want your children to understand your love for Jesus, share the music you love with them.

I urge you to examine your musical diet. Consider consuming the spiritual food that will keep your relationship with God and others healthy. Help yourself to some spiritual jam when you need to make the hard stuff easier to swallow. It will take some work to change your habits. But it's well worth the effort in order to walk daily with the Lord, to give thanks in all things, and to be obedient to the authority over you. Singing Christian music in your heart will help you to do these things.

Do you feel the good dog and bad dog wrestling in your life? Christian music feeds the good dog, and it replenishes your faith and joy. It's much more important than you may know. But now that you're beginning to discover what Christian music can do for you, it's time to think about what kind of Christian music you should listen to. ♩

Chapter 13

WHAT DOES CHRISTIAN MUSIC SOUND LIKE?

"He put a new song in my mouth."
(Psalm 40:3)

It was one of those rare occasions when I could afford to go out with friends for a steak dinner. When our order arrived, I was struck by the variety of our choices. We all had gotten steak, but we had different ideas about how it should be seasoned. Two people used only salt and pepper. Another used A-1 Sauce. To the embarrassment of the group's gourmet, one even put ketchup on his steak! I had ordered *carne asada* (steak with hot sauce).

Why didn't we all season our steaks the same? Because we each had different tastes. The ones who seasoned their steaks with salt and pepper thought I was nuts for eating mine with hot sauce. "Why cover the natural taste?" they asked. I explained that I was simply enhancing my enjoyment of steak with my favorite spice, just as they were.

They were from Minnesota and I was from San Diego, so they had a hard time understanding why anyone would put hot sauce on a steak. But what they call hot sauce in the Midwest, we call ketchup in southern California! My family can eat some types of hot sauce by the spoonful, yet the same sauce raises blisters on the tongues of my Minnesota-bred in-laws.

Our assortment of seasonings reminded me of a lot of discussions I've had with Christians over the proper "flavor" of music. Depending on whom you talk to, musical tastes include classical, country, contemporary, jazz, marching tunes, or big bands. *Why doesn't every Christian like the same style of music?* Because everyone has different tastes. It is natural for people of different ages who live in various geographic locations to have a variety of tastes in many aspects of their lives, including music.

After my steak dinner, I recalled two other memorable meals. One took place several summers ago when I took a group of Japanese exchange students to a local Mexican restaurant. (What better way to introduce Japanese people to American culture than by feeding them Mexican food!) Some of us suggested they try the special tostadas. But instead of devouring them, as I had anticipated, the students politely picked at their meals and ate only a little lettuce and some rice. Why? I found out that the Japanese usually don't use spices on their food. These students were from the country that gave us the delicacy of sushi—raw fish! A Mexican restaurant was definitely not the place for them.

The other meal I remembered had been equally educational for me. A neighbor from India invited some people for dinner to treat us to the food of his homeland. If you think Mexican food is hot, try food seasoned with Indian curry. It was so hot it made my eyeballs sweat! I drank a lot of water that evening. And to my chagrin, the very meal that was steaming out my nose was being enjoyed by most of the Indian guests. To this day I can't eat food spiced with curry. It's a taste I've never acquired.

These dining experiences leave us with the question of which country correctly seasons its food: mellow Japan, spicy Mexico, or red-hot India? The answer, of course, is that one is not especially right nor another particularly wrong. Each is simply different. And the enjoyment of any specific kind of food is rooted in personal taste.

Now let's change our focus from food to music. *Which style is best: mellow, spicy (upbeat, contemporary, rock), or somewhere in between?* Again, the answer is that one is no more correct than another. Each style of music is simply different. A person's choice of music depends on his cultural background, maturity and age, the music he grew up listening to, and his personal tastes.

Is there a limit as to how spicy our musical steak should be? While the Bible speaks specifically about the importance of spiritual music in our lives (Psalm 96:1, 2; Ephesians 5:19; Colossians 3:16), it never describes the kind of seasoning that "steak" is to have. Just as we are given the freedom to have different tastes in regard to food, we also have the freedom to have different tastes when it comes to music.

Some Christians will inevitably choose hot sauce to season their musical steak. They may simply prefer that spice, but there are also good reasons for choosing spicier music. It not only satisfies a different taste; it serves a different purpose.

Other Christians prefer older hymns and mellow worship music, and certainly no one can argue with this choice of spice. Traditional music is extremely relevant today, especially when we need to encourage an attitude of prayer and worship. But we don't need to limit ourselves to only one type of seasoning for our spiritual steaks.

THE BASICS

We have already seen that the foundation of Christian music is to be psalms, hymns, and spiritual songs. These categories bring to mind mellow music. In fact, critics of contemporary Christian music often present this argument: "The Bible says to sing psalms, hymns, and spiritual songs. The psalms and hymns I know are mellow. Contemporary Christian music isn't mellow, so it must be wrong."

Is this thinking logical? Is it biblical? *Is there a proper place in the Christian life for spicy music?* We need to consider two things when examining "spice" on musical steak: volume and tension. Upon hearing contemporary Christian music, critics will often claim that the volume is too loud to be spiritual. *But exactly how loud is too loud? Is soft music more biblical than loud music? At what volume does it go from being spiritual to unspiritual?*

In my studies of Scripture, I have yet to find a command that we should sing softly or quietly to God. Not one. Yet in casual reading of Scripture—especially Psalms—I have found dozens of instructions to sing loudly, play musical instruments loudly, and generally make a loud noise to praise God. Over the years I have remarked that if we are quiet in our singing and playing to God, we are missing out. I never realized how true that was until I began to examine the meanings of some of the original Hebrew words.

In the Bible, four different Hebrew words are translated as "singing." *Zamar* refers to singing while playing a stringed instrument. *Shuwr* gives the sense of singing while strolling along, as a singing minstrel would. The other two, *ranan* and *ruwa,* indicate that the singing should be loud. One-quarter to one-third of the Scriptures that refer to singing indicate that it should be loud.

Just how loud? The root of *ranan* suggests that the singing should be a loud, raspy, harsh-sounding shrill. The root of *ruwa* suggests that the singing should split the ears with sound! So the next time we start to criticize a Christian band for being too loud, we should remember Scripture. Maybe, they're just doing what the Bible says to do!

Another area of contemporary Christian music we need to examine is the element of tension. People often point out that contemporary Christian music is not relaxing and does not encourage an attitude of worship. I agree. But is that reason enough to pronounce that this music is wrong? I don't believe so.

Something happened in our home one night that taught me about the proper use of tension. I have two teenage daughters who love the Lord and are not openly rebellious. A few years ago, as they were playing a game on the floor, the buzzer on the dryer indicated that the clothes were ready to come out. My wife, Jan, and I were reading on the sofa. Jan looked up from her reading and said in her usual calm voice, "Ann, I'm really tired. The clothes are done. I want you to bring them in here and fold them. Is that clear?"

My daughter nodded and said, "Yes."

My wife went back to her reading. The girls went back to their game. Five minutes later the wrinkleguard feature on the dryer kicked in, turned the clothes a few more times, and again the buzzer blared out that the clothes were done. At that point, my wife noticed that Ann hadn't moved. She slowly and deliberately put down the paper and looked over at our daughter. "Ann," she said, "I thought I asked you to get the clothes."

Ann, who is normally very obedient, looked up with her sweet innocent face and said, "I didn't know you meant now." Jan stared her straight in the eye with a look that could cut steel, and said sternly, "I'm really tired. The clothes are done. I want you to bring them in here and fold them. Is that clear?" She didn't raise her voice. She didn't get angry. But each word was punctuated with a tension that said, "You'd better move now or you're in big trouble!" Ann got up immediately and took care of the laundry.

My wife repeated the exact same words to my daughter. The first time her voice didn't have any tension in it.

But simply by changing her tone of voice, she added an element of urgency to her command. We all use different tones of voice for various situations when dealing with our children. We don't say, "Let's pray," with the same amount of tension as, "Let's clean up that room!"

Do you think our Lord used the same tone of voice to say "Suffer the little children to come unto me," and "My father's house is not a den of thieves"? Of course not. The first statement was soft, gentle, and full of assurance. The second was very tense and urgent. It called for an immediate response from those in the temple.

The same distinctions can be made about Christian music. One style of music may be calm and conducive to praise and worship. Another may express an urgency that demands action. Musicians often express a variety of moods with various styles of music.

This principle is further emphasized in 2 Timothy 3:16 where we are told that, "All Scripture is God-breathed and is useful for teaching, rebuking, correcting and training in righteousness." Since Christian music is simply Scripture and scriptural principles set to a tune, it too should be used to teach, reprove, correct, and train in righteousness. Naturally, rebuke and correction require a more urgent tone than comfort or encouragement.

Much contemporary Christian music is basically saying, "Live out your faith! NOW!" It teaches, rebukes, corrects, and trains with a tone that communicates a call to action. It has tension. And it contains three elements consistently associated with rock music: passion, action, and urgency. The obvious distinction is that most secular music says, "Do whatever you want! I mean it! Do it NOW!" In contrast, contemporary Christian music says, "Live for Jesus! I mean it! Do it NOW!"

Many people say that the nature of rock music is immoral, but this isn't exactly true. Yes, the nature of rock music is to be passionate and energetic, and to communicate urgency with tension. But until we examine the lyrics and the lifestyles of the performers, we aren't certain what to be passionate about. Rock-and-roll musicians have been passionate about sex and self for so long, people have begun to assume rock music is always sexual, selfish, and sinful—in and of itself. But that isn't always the case.

Rock music communicates energy, emotion, a mood. The words and performers then give content and direction to that mood. Christian music can communicate with the same energy as secular rock, but the words and performers can give that energy a completely new focus—living for Jesus Christ.

Music has many uses in the Christian life. It is not only designed for the purpose of worship. It can teach and disciple. It can challenge and relate to the hurting world. It can reflect joy and triumph, passion and urgency, rage and fear, guilt and repentance—just as the psalmists did. To do this, music requires a variety of styles, sounds, volumes, and moods. We must learn to determine which style of music—active or passive, intense or relaxed—best fits each situation and emotion.

BUT WHAT ABOUT...?

Some people are wary about listening to contemporary Christian music because, "I heard that there is a specific beat that is demonic." The theory of a "demon beat" was generated from a story about a missionary's daughter in Java who played contemporary Christian music. One native, a recent convert to Christianity, told the missionaries that their daughter's album had the same beat that he had previously used in pagan worship.

I didn't believe the story when I first heard it. The conclusions seemed ludicrous. A specific beat that would call up demons? The windshield wipers on my 82 VW had a similar beat. Would I get poor gas mileage? If I tapped my foot a specific way, would I become possessed? It just didn't make sense to me. But many Bible-believing Christians were basing their opinions about contemporary Christian music on this story, so I decided to investigate.

I checked with the office of the conference leader who first told the story. They gave me the name and address of the son of the missionaries. I got in touch with him and asked him to verify the story. He confirmed that in 1971, an older native had indeed told them the music his sister was listening to was similar to music used in pagan worship.

I was so intrigued with the story that I found a copy of the offending album. It is titled, *Sounds of a New Generation!* It was produced by Youth for Christ/Campus Life in the early 70s and featured performers like Cliff Barrows, The Spurlows, Ralph Carmichael, and others. The songs included "It's Free" (with a smooth calypso beat), "When the Roll Is Called Up Yonder," and one of the most beautiful renditions I've ever heard of "He's Everything to Me."

In case you are not familiar with that last song, it was written by Ralph Carmichael in 1963. It is a wonderful song of praise to God, and the beat would never make me think of chanting natives or even a frenzied rock band. I'm not able to dispute the old native gentleman, but if this song is demonic, nearly every Christian choir in America must be in danger. The song has been popular in Bible-believing fundamental Christian churches for nearly three decades.

Either the native misinterpreted what he heard or millions of born-again Christians are being ministered to by demon-possessed music—which is not possible. We would have to eliminate Steve Green, the Gaithers,

Michael Card, and many of the children's musicals and gospel quartets from our music collections.

So how do we respond to the missionary's story? I believe the native confused the passion connected to his former style of worship with the passion of the Christian music. Remember, passion can be used for good as well as evil.

Another objection people mention in regard to contemporary Christian music is that the artists imitate the "worldly" look of rock and roll. At my Christian music seminars, many of the adults are introduced to contemporary Christian music for the first time. One middle-aged mother approached me after a seminar and asked, "Those young singers may love Jesus and sing for His glory, but why do they have to look and sound like the world?" My response was simple: "What does the world look and sound like?"

Does the world sound more like Pearl Jam or Harry Connick, Jr.? What sound do you think is the most worldly: pop? rock? country? rap? hardcore? blues? punk? jazz? If you think Christian music is okay as long as it sounds like Glenn Miller (Garth Brooks? Aretha Franklin?), does that mean you believe those music styles are not worldly? Could a romantic ballad be just as hedonistic and immoral as a wild party rock tune? Christian music often resembles secular music in style, but the Christian musicians I know have by no means conformed to the world (Romans 12:1, 2). Their hearts belong to Jesus Christ.

But why do Christian musicians have to look like their worldly counterparts? First of all, let me say that the vast majority of contemporary Christian artists look and dress normally. A few have longer hair and wear weird-looking clothes, which seems to shake up some of the people in the Christian community. But can you truly say they are conforming to the world just because their clothes are strange to you? Who is to say that God finds their appearance offensive, and not yours or mine?

We know without question that suggestive and sensual clothes are inappropriate for a Christian. Christians should dress with modesty in mind (1 Timothy 2:9, 10; 1 Peter 3:3, 4). It is sinful for a man to dress in a way that would make him appear as if he wanted to be a woman, or for a woman to try to look like a man. But to go beyond these biblical standards and insist that it is sinful for Christian musicians to look like secular musicians brings up some other questions.

Why limit this criticism to musicians? In our society, the love of materialism is promoted by many Wall Street executives in three-piece business suits. We know that this love of materialism is a value system that God detests (Matthew 6:24). Yet the Christian church readily accepts and encourages an identification with the suit-and-tie image. Are Christian executives guilty of identifying in appearance with a value system that God hates?

Who is conforming more to the world in their appearance, Christian musicians or Christian executives? Who's to say that a Christian artist who dresses "weird" isn't consciously trying to avoid identification with a materialistic value system? In our diligence to live up to holy standards, let's be careful to make sure our guidelines are biblical. We must be careful about judging others based on appearance and never forget that, "'The LORD does not look at the things man looks at. Man looks at the outward appearance, but the LORD looks at the heart'" (1 Samuel 16:7).

Other critics of contemporary Christian music accuse the musicians of teaching a shallow gospel. Their accusations are usually unfounded, but even if they are right about the music, it is still their biblical responsibility to support and accept their weaker brothers (Romans 14:1-8). Let me share a situation that relates to this.

My staff and I review just about every Christian album that is produced. I once evaluated an album that I thought had the spiritual depth of a 10 year old. I was ready to dump the tape in the trash when I realized I *had* a 10 year old. So I gave it to my daughter, and she loved it.

If good Christian music is steak, then this tape was pabulum—baby food. But baby food meets a definite need for babies. And spiritual babies will benefit from spiritual baby food. If you criticize a baby for acting like a baby, he'll never grow to want steak (Hebrews 5:12-14).

It is futile to expect a young child to live up to all the mature standards of a Christian adult. Trying to force a child into this mold only creates resentment, anger, and ultimately, a sense of failure. We need to meet children where they are and help them in a steady climb to maturity. There is no better tool for the task than Christian music.

SOME CAUTIONS

So are we to accept any kind of music that claims to be Christian? Aren't there any limitations or guidelines we should look for? As a matter of fact, there are several cautions and biblical guidelines we need to keep in mind.

First, we must remember that freedom to choose is not a license to indulge ourselves: "'Everything is permissible for me'—but not everything is beneficial. 'Everything is permissible for me'—but I will not be mastered by anything" (1 Corinthians 6:12). Just because God allows us some choices in which spices we prefer, we would be unwise to float the steak in the seasoning. Spices should be used to enhance the true flavor of the meat. To hide the meat in the spice is to render the Word of God useless in our lives.

What good is a message if it can't be understood? The message of most Christian songs is in the lyrics. But what if the listener is too enchanted with the beautiful melody, too absorbed in how much fun the beat is, or too frustrated because the volume is too loud? If any aspect of the music draws him away from the truth of the message, the song becomes less effective in strengthening his faith and joy.

But with this in mind, we also need to be careful about telling people what kind of music will or won't minister to them. I often think back to the late 70s when I thought I knew what kind of Christian music everybody should listen to. Since I was "spiritual," I assumed that everybody else who was spiritual should listen to the music I liked. I got by with this attitude for quite awhile.

Then one day a pastor at a church where I was speaking told me I couldn't recommend Keith Green's music. At the time, I was (and still am) deeply challenged and motivated to godly living by his music. When I asked the pastor why he objected, he said it was because Keith Green's music didn't minister to him and he didn't see how it could minister to anyone else.

In deference to that pastor's authority, I did not recommend Keith Green's music that night. But I remember asking myself, *"When did God die and leave this guy in charge? How could he possibly say that music that ministers to me is wrong? Who is he to climb into my soul and determine what ministers to me?"* Then I started to realize that I had been doing the same thing to other people for years! Since I knew what ministered to me, I tried to tell others what should minister to them. How foolish. The Bible is full of warnings about trying to judge other people. Yet that's exactly what I had been doing— attempting to climb into their souls and tell them what kind of Christian music would minister to them.

We must be very cautious when we presume to make musical evaluations for others. It may still be our responsibility to guide, advise, or choose for others, especially our children. But our personal tastes are not the final guideline. Our final test is whether the message of the music is against biblical values. If it is against biblical values, go to Scripture and point out the contradiction.

So what kind of "spice" should you put on your "steak"? It depends on your purpose for listening. Personally, I like to start and end my day with an attitude of worship. During those times, my music is lightly seasoned with little or no tension. The same is true when I'm studying or trying to concentrate on a project. But when I'm working in the yard or driving my car, I like to crank up the tempo with a lot of "spice." In its own way, each music style helps me focus on life from God's point of view.

I am not writing this book to persuade you to enjoy what I enjoy. I am not trying to promote one style of Christian music over any other. I'm not suggesting the best style of music for the Christian. I'm simply saying that God recognizes the freedom of personal taste in this matter, and so should His people.

If Christian music ministers to your spirit, listen to it. If it doesn't, find some that will. There is plenty out there to choose from.

Chapter 14

CULTIVATING A TASTE FOR CHRISTIAN MUSIC IN YOUR CHILD

*"Even a child is known by his actions, by
whether his conduct is pure and right."
(Proverbs 20:11)*

Occasionally at a seminar, even before I have begun my presentation, a concerned parent will come up to me and say something like, "I don't know what you're going to say, but I'm sure I'll believe you. Just don't spend a lot of time telling me rock music is wrong, because I already know that. I can see the effects on my children. What I want to know is what I can do about it."

A lot of parents have heard seminars on rock music before. They already understand that much of today's music can be evil. They don't want their children listening to it, yet they don't know what to do. Parents need practical help to deal with the issue in their homes. It is not enough to expose the sins and shortcomings of secular rock. They want some real hope for their families.

Consequently, I have been challenged to refocus my ministry. Now I do much more speaking targeted to adults rather than young people. I deeply feel the need to reach parents with biblical principles and workable answers pertaining to rock music. The guidelines in this book are a result of my work with concerned parents.

I've tried to develop a step-by-step process that deals with the real issues in the music world today.

You must communicate a real love for your children along with your concern about their entertainment. You need to take the time to examine your child's secular music and help him see how it influences his faith and joy in Jesus Christ. You need to be willing to examine your own life and entertainment to ensure that your faith and joy are all that God wants them to be. And you need to understand how to cultivate a heart for God using Christian music.

This book has already addressed most of these areas, yet one basic question remains: *How can I get my family interested in listening to Christian music?* Let me share a few ideas to get you started. (Some of these ideas have been mentioned previously, yet they bear repeating in this context.)

1. START ON YOUR KNEES

If you understood the steps presented in chapter eleven, then you know why prayer needs to be the first step in every area of managing our families. This fact cannot be emphasized strongly enough. Don't get so caught up with your own concerns that you don't take time to seriously pray for your children. If you're too busy to pray, you're just too busy.

2. SET CHRISTIAN ENTERTAINMENT GUIDELINES FOR YOUR FAMILY

Sit down with your spouse (or another concerned adult, if you are a single parent) and outline some guidelines for Christian entertainment in your home. What types of Christian music will you allow your children to listen to? What will not be allowed? Try to be open-minded and include the widest selection of Christian music styles possible, but don't go beyond what you honestly think is appropriate for your children. As a parent, you have every right and responsibility to say, "I don't care if that *is* Christian music, I don't want you to listen to it." (But be careful of saying that God doesn't like it just because you don't.)

Once you have established a general outline, discuss it with your children. Ask for their input. Establish a regular time to sit down with them and discuss the ministry value of their music. Be willing to be flexible. Remember, the idea is not to force our tastes on our children, but to help them choose a saving faith in Christ, be excited about Christianity, and grow stronger in their relationship to God.

3. SET A CONSISTENT EXAMPLE

Evaluate your own example in the light of God's Word. What are your favorite forms of entertainment? If they reflect the same secular philosophies your children are choosing, then don't expect to see your children change without a fight. Do you regularly listen to and express enthusiasm about Christian music? Does your family see you willing to choose the things of God, or do they detect a bit of reluctance? Examine the example you are setting. It is most effective when it is faithful, consistent, truthful, and joyful.

4. TEACH WITHOUT JUDGING

Despite the fact that you may criticize some of their secular music, be sure your children understand that you are not critical of them. Make sure they see you are challenging them to do something positive. It isn't enough to criticize your children's choice of music and complain about things that are wrong. You must motivate them to take actions that are wholesome and good. Parents who don't understand this will be defeated.

It is tempting for parents to assume that if their children conform to parental ideals, that's good enough. When it comes to spiritual issues, parents are often afraid to let their children think for themselves. We must teach our children how to think, not just what to think. If they don't learn how to think through spiritual issues as they are growing up, they certainly won't know how as adults.

5.   DISCUSS THE MINISTRY VALUE OF CHRISTIAN MUSIC WITH YOUR CHILDREN

Christian music that ministers to parents will not automatically minister to their children. And not everything called "Christian music" will encourage all people in the same way. Parents need to discuss the ministry and messages of the Christian music their children listen to. They must ask some challenging questions that will help young people evaluate their music on a spiritual level.

The first basic question should be, *"How is your faith and joy?"* Thoroughly explore together what this question means. Don't be superficial. Do some digging in God's Word together. You might be surprised to discover what your child really thinks. Instead of judging his music, stick to the real issue of faith and joy. Since so much secular rock music opposes what Christ has taught, a steady diet of it will certainly undermine a person's faith and joy.

Another important question is, *"Does your music minister to you as a believer?"* This question challenges your child to think and reply. Wait for a response: "Yes,"

"No," or "I don't know" (which counts as a no). Even though the child may say yes, you may not be convinced. Don't hesitate to ask for specifics as to how the music ministers. Just be careful to assure your children that you love and accept them, regardless of their taste in music.

This is the time to offer your opinions and concerns about their music. Guide them through this stage by pointing out philosophies that are against biblical values. Distinguish between your personal tastes in music and God's principles for life in Scripture. If they can show that their music is honestly spiritual and significant, let it be. Allow the Holy Spirit to use the music to build your child's faith and joy.

If your children cannot show that their music is beneficial to their spiritual lives, you need to help them begin to find Christian music that will build up their faith and joy. Be willing to invest in Christian music for your children—not according to *your* taste, but based on what will minister to *them.*

6. INVEST IN A TAPE DECK OR CD PLAYER FOR YOUR CAR

Even if you are convinced you should listen to Christian music, you may find that there is no Christian radio station in your area. But don't give up just because it isn't convenient to listen to Christian music. If it is important enough, you will find a way to get it done.

Since most people spend so much time driving, start by investing in a tape or CD player for your car. Otherwise you tend to gravitate back to the secular music on the car radio. When you listen to Christian recordings, you have more control of the environment. For one thing, it eliminates the contests to see who gets to select the radio station.

I always have at least two tapes in my car, ready to play when we travel as a family. One tape is quiet background music that will allow for conversation. The other one is more suited for focusing on the messages in the songs. When we're driving, it's Christian music or nothing. (By the way, driving without any music is an ideal opportunity to follow the Lord's challenge to "'Be still, and know that I am God'" [Psalm 46:10].)

7. BUY A SMALL CASSETTE PLAYER FOR YOUR CHILDREN

Play mellow Christian music for your children when you put them to bed and as they get ready for school. (Make sure the recorder has an "automatic off" feature so it will turn off when the tape finishes playing.) We've done this since the day our first daughter was born. Christian music has a remarkably calming effect at bedtime and helps set a positive tone for the day as children get dressed for school. Without realizing it, our children have memorized Scripture and scriptural principles as they listened again and again to the songs we have played.

As they have grown older, we have given them more input as to the choice of music. If they are well behaved and go to bed easily, they get to pick the tape to be played. If not, I choose a suitable selection. It's a win/win situation.

While she was growing up, my younger daughter and I had a contest. If she stayed awake through the first side of a tape, she could call me to turn it over. Most of the time she was asleep before that happened. It was a thrill for me as a daddy to know that her last thoughts before she fell asleep were about the things of God.

Another excellent investment you can make is for a portable Walkman-type tape player for each child. With no radio to divert their attention, they can spend hours listening to their favorite Christian tapes. Long trips in the car also become much calmer when children can listen to their own choice of music.

8. SUPPORT YOUR LOCAL CHRISTIAN RADIO STATION

Contemporary Christian music radio stations are becoming more common across the country. Find out if there is such a station in your area and then look for ways that its ministry can influence your family life. Many people are not aware of the various Christian influences in their communities, including radio/TV stations, newspapers, bookstores, or other inspirational resources.

If your local Christian radio station doesn't play songs you enjoy, make requests. Express your opinion to station management, because most stations want to play what the market is listening for. If the station is nonprofit, consider giving it financial support. It is a ministry that can reach today's generation in a language they will appreciate.

9. ENCOURAGE MUSICAL TALENT IN CHILDREN

When children have the chance to make music come to life, they will never forget it. This can be done through school band, private lessons, or participation in church musicals. You will enjoy it, too! Some families create their own Christian music by taking Scripture passages or original lyrics and setting them to music. Each member of the family has his own instrument—store-bought or homemade. What a great project for the family! You may discover a wealth of hidden talent in your children when you encourage them to make music in the home.

10. ATTEND CHRISTIAN CONCERTS/ MUSICALS AS A FAMILY

It is important to help your children see that Christian music is also for adults. Watch for local Christian concerts through your church, Christian radio station, bookstore, or newspaper. Occasionally let your children choose a concert to attend. Try several different kinds of music. If you don't happen to like the artist or group someone else selects, be honest enough to express your concerns with them. Be specific, but also be careful not to indict a whole category of music because of one unpleasant incident.

Remember, your taste in spice will probably be somewhat different than theirs. At first, your children may enjoy a concert only for its entertainment value. It will be up to you to help them understand the ministry value of the music by discussing how the singer's message applies to their lives.

11. INVEST IN CHRISTIAN MUSIC FOR YOUR HOME

Use any excuse to buy your children Christian music! Christmas and birthdays are naturals, but don't overlook other opportunities such as good report cards, poor report cards, or losing a tooth! Any reason is a good reason to give Christian music. Yes, this habit can be expensive, but it's worth the investment. You are investing in the spiritual life and character of each of your children. Investments pay dividends! The dividends you'll see in your family are children who love God and have a deeper understanding of His Word.

These ways to interest children in Christian music have already worked for a lot of parents. I hope you will want to incorporate some or all of these suggestions. There is no need to let music destroy your family. Instead, use it as a mirror to examine the soul of your child. Let it be a means by which you share your love for Jesus. Consider it a tool to help shape your children into a Christlike image. And most of all, use it to help you and your family focus on the glory of God.

COMMUNICATING SPIRITUAL VALUES USING MUSIC

*"These commandments that I give you
today are to be upon your hearts.
Impress them on your children."
(Deuteronomy 6:6, 7)*

At a major evangelical church in northern California, I was challenging the congregation to incorporate Christian music into their everyday lives at home. To communicate a point to the parents, I said to the youth, "Kids, fill in the blank. Christian music is _____." With one voice, they answered, "Boring!"

The parents couldn't believe it. You could see it on their faces: "Not only do our children listen to the enemy's music, but they think our music is boring. With this attitude, how are we ever going to get them to listen to Christian music?"

These families were in one of the largest and strongest Christian churches in that area, and I get the same response at most other churches where I speak. Adults everywhere tend to assume that new Christians and young people automatically enjoy traditional church music. It has never occurred to many church parents that it takes time and effort to teach young people to value and enjoy Christian music.

Jesus once described a man who cast a demon out of his house. Then he cleaned his house and put it in order, but left it unattended. The empty, unguarded house was filled with seven demons when he returned, and his condition was worse than ever (Luke 11:24-26). It is not enough to simply remove the demons of rock music. We must fill the void with something positive and equally dynamic.

I have seen many people, young and old, decide to throw out their secular music, but then reverse their decisions later on. And when they do go back to secular music, they are usually even more devoted to it. Their intentions were good, but they didn't find a positive replacement for the music they gave up.

As a child begins to let go of secular music and media, parents must make a definite effort to fill the void left. We would do well to review Deuteronomy 6:7, which instructs us to use every opportunity to teach children the commandments of God. We are to impress them on our children. We are to discuss them when we are at home, as we walk along the road, when we lie down, and when we get up.

This can be very convicting. Many church families do not think much about God, and they may actually be focusing on the things of Satan through their choice of entertainment. When they sit at home, they absorb empty philosophies through television or secular music. When they go along the road, they cruise to the emptiness blasting from their car stereos. When they lie down and get up, their clock radios focus on the values of this present age instead of the age to come.

How do we get our families to change their focus? How do we get our kids to focus their minds about the things of God if they believe Christian music is boring? We must teach the value of Christian music. It is our responsibility as parents to convince our children that

Christian music can be exciting and dynamic, and that the gospel it presents can cut like a two-edged sword.

SHARING YOUR TESTIMONY SONG

There is hope. One way to cultivate a taste for Christian music is through a testimony song. This is a song that expresses your love for God and describes your walk with the Lord. It doesn't necessarily express who God is or describe the great things that He does. Rather, it should be a song that expresses how you personally feel about your relationship with God. A testimony song lets someone else understand why you love Jesus. Every Christian should have a testimony song.

Select a song that accurately describes the feelings you have in your soul for Jesus, not one you think your children will like. You aren't likely to find a true testimony song that will also entertain your children. A mature adult and a young child rarely have the same taste in music.

My first testimony song was "Heaven Came Down and Glory Filled My Soul." The first time I heard it, I got all excited. I thought, *"That's it! That's exactly what happened to me in 1971 when I committed my life to Jesus."* It was like Heaven came down and glory filled my soul!

Several years later I heard a B. J. Thomas song called "He Gave Me Love When No One Gave Me a Prayer." It made me recall my spiritual struggle during the time after my mother was hospitalized. Remember, all my Christian friends had given up on me and quit praying for me. And my mother was too sick to pray for me as she had for so long. But God, in His mercy and grace, chose to love me and save me anyway. God gave me love when (literally) no one gave me a prayer.

That song illustrated my past, but I also like to look to my future. My children are my future. When I heard the song "Somewhere in the World" on the *Giants in the Land* album by Wayne Watson, it became my most inspiring testimony song. The challenge of the song is to pray for the person your child will marry someday. This is something my wife and I have done ever since our daughters were toddlers.

Why pray for their future husbands even while our daughters are little girls? Because somewhere in the world those future husbands—whoever they are—are little boys. With the pressures to conform to this world, those little boys need a lot of prayer. If it's tough to have a successful marriage now, imagine how difficult it will be by the time they are adults. I want my daughters to live for Jesus as adults and to have successful marriages. Wayne Watson's song reminds me to keep praying. Even though I don't know who I'm praying for, God does.

Don't pick your song too quickly. Many parents want to choose a favorite hymn because it's familiar and easy. But I would like to challenge you to listen to a lot of different Christian songs and artists. Listen until you find one that precisely expresses your love for Jesus.

When you find an appropriate song, ask your kids for five minutes of their time. Explain that you would like to have them listen to a song that means a lot to you. Take one of your five minutes to give a little background and why you chose this song. Then have them read the lyrics with you while the song is played. Make sure they focus on the message of the song instead of its sound. Do your best to make this a pleasant experience, and don't force participation if you haven't been communicating well up to this point.

The goal is to allow your family to share what you feel in your soul and to see your love for Jesus. Follow the song with a question or two. Don't ask, "Did you like that?" or "Wasn't that cool?" Ask instead, "Now do you understand why I love Jesus?" or "Do you understand a little more about why I am a Christian? This is very important to me."

This exercise can accomplish a number of things. First, it shows your children at least one Christian song that isn't boring. The music may not have been their favorite style, but they begin to see Christian music as something personal, deep, and interesting. This may be a new experience for them.

Second, you model vulnerability by exposing your innermost spiritual feelings to your child. If you're ever going to introduce your children to Jesus, they have to understand why you love Him. Be willing to discuss any issues that arise from listening to your testimony song. Be prepared to extend the five minutes to as long as it takes to answer questions and finish the discussion.

Third, children often begin to think of songs that speak personally to them. Whenever I give this challenge during a seminar, many people begin to think through their library of songs for one that explains their love for Jesus. Your children are likely to have the same response.

Finally, your child will subconsciously learn to evaluate his own music for ministry value. Previously, he may have thought of music simply as a means of entertainment. Now he will begin to understand that music can be more. It can also be ministry. When this happens, you are getting through the spice to the steak.

By the way, these principles can easily be applied in a group setting. I hear from pastors, Christian school-teachers, youth workers, Sunday school teachers, and others who have utilized the principles and techniques of the testimony song with great success.

CHRISTIAN MUSIC AS A TEACHING TOOL

Christian music can be a springboard to launch all sorts of discussions about personal and spiritual values with young people. It can help us talk to our children, listen to them, understand them better, and help them work through the values, morals, and spiritual issues in their lives. Parents and other caring adults want to communicate with children, but find it difficult to relate to a younger generation. That's why I encourage adults to use Christian music as a communication tool.

Studies show that the average father offers his children less than five minutes of effective communication each day. Mothers average only slightly more. The problem may not be that the parents don't want to communicate with their children. Maybe they don't know how, because sometimes it can be like pulling teeth.

I have to be honest. I don't have much in common with my daughters. They're girls and I'm not. They're teenagers and I'm middle-aged. I do my very best to develop common interests, but sometimes they just don't want to talk. Sometimes they don't believe I'm going to listen anyway. Sometimes I don't ask the right questions. Sometimes I talk about things that interest me rather than things that interest them. But I keep trying.

My desire is to be better than the average father who talks to his child less than five minutes a day. Sometimes when I get lax, my wife challenges me, "Al, why don't you put in your five minutes today?" So I pick up my daughters at school, ready and eager to communicate. I remember a conversation I had with one of them when she was in elementary school. It went like this:

"Hi, Allison. Did you have fun today?"

"Yes."

"What did you do?"

"Played."

"Oh. Well, what did you do besides play?"

"Schoolwork."

"Well, tell me, what's the first thing you did?"

"Studied the Bible."

"Which part?"

"About Daniel."

"What did you learn about Daniel?"

"Lions' den."

"How about math?"

"We did arithmetic."

"What did you learn in arithmetic?"

"Fractions."

"What did you learn about fractions?"

"We learned what a numerator and a denominator was."

"What else are you studying?"

"Missions in California history."

"What about the missions?"

"San Diego was the first."

This exchange was an actual conversation. I consider myself to be above average in communication skills. In fact, my ministry depends on my ability to communicate. But I've come to realize that the only thing I have in common with my children is that we all love their mother.

Thankfully, I have found that I don't have to depend on "out of the blue" conversations to communicate with my daughters. I have discovered how to use Christian music to initiate some wonderful times of discussion. Sharing Christian music with my daughters has helped me understand how they think, how they feel, and who they are. I have seen sides of them I never saw before. I have been able to discuss things with them that I would have no idea how to bring up otherwise. I have been able to talk about spiritual truth in very natural ways.

Actually, I discovered this quite by accident. When my older daughter was six, we were in the car listening to a Leslie Phillips song from her album, *Beyond Saturday Night*. The song was called "Gina." Leslie sang about her friend Gina, who had been killed in an automobile accident before Leslie had a chance to tell her about Jesus.

I didn't realize that Ann was listening, but suddenly she said, "Daddy, does that mean that Gina went to Hell?"

Ann's question hit me like a ton of bricks. I was stunned. I had to say, "Yes, if she didn't know Jesus, the Bible tells us she would go to Hell."

"Why didn't Leslie tell Gina about Jesus, if she knew Gina was going to Hell if she died?" Ann asked.

"Well," I said, "I guess Leslie figured that she had more time, but actually she didn't." At that point, I was able to talk to my daughter about Heaven and Hell, along with other important things from the Word of God.

Our conversation had a dramatic effect on how my daughter related to others. From that point on she wouldn't play long with new friends before asking them, "Do you know Jesus? Do you go to church? Are you a Christian?" She was afraid that her friends might die before she told them about Jesus.

Our conversation also had a dramatic impact on me. I realized that I could discuss life-changing issues with my daughters through music. Ann was willing to listen because she brought up the topic. Who knows if she listens when I try to lecture at her? But with music as the catalyst, I had a wonderful opportunity to talk to her about significant issues. Since then, Christian music has led to many other opportunities to communicate God's truth to both my daughters.

LEVELS OF MATURITY

But playing Christian music doesn't automatically guarantee good communication. Sometimes it takes a little work. A few years later, I was on a speaking tour, traveling with my family in a motor home. While we were driving through the Midwestern plains, we happened to be listening to a Russ Taff song from his *Medals* album called, "Not Gonna Bow." I was enjoying it, pleased to be a neat Christian father encouraging my neat little Christian daughters to listen to this neat Christian music, which I knew had a tremendous spiritual message.

"Ann," I said, "do you like that song?"

"Yes," she replied.

"Do you know what it means?"

She looked at me and said, "No."

That's when it hit me. I was listening to a song's spiritual content and being ministered to. But I was a mature adult. My daughter, who was spiritually less mature, was listening only because it had a sound that she enjoyed. She didn't understand the message.

What should a father do in a case like that? Should he criticize his daughter for listening to music just because she likes the sound? Or does he take that opportunity to explain the message to her? I chose the latter. I began explaining the spiritual significance of "Not Gonna Bow." I reviewed the story of Shadrach, Meshach, and Abednego mentioned in the song.

The song tells how a young boy named Bobby was asked to compromise his faith by giving in to the things of the world. All his friends said, "Come on, Bobby, won't you be like us? Come on, Bobby, what's the fuss?"

But Bobby said, "No, I'm not gonna bow."

I explained to Ann how the experience of Shadrach, Meshach, and Abednego applied to Bobby's situation at his school. Then we talked about ways the song could apply to peer-pressure situations in her life. After she understood the message, that song became her favorite.

Not long after that, Ann came home from school on a rainy day which had been spent almost entirely indoors. To pass the time during the lunch hour, the teacher had her pupils ask different questions. One little girl had asked, "How many watch MTV?"

Ann reported, "Everybody raised their hand but me."

I asked, "Why didn't you raise your hand?"

She replied, "Because I don't watch MTV."

"Ann," I said, "that's nice. I'm very proud of you."

"But, Daddy," she said, "Mary raised her hand, and she doesn't watch MTV either."

"Honey," I said, "why do you suppose Mary raised her hand?"

"Because she was probably afraid everybody would laugh at her."

I said, "You're probably right. So why didn't you raise your hand?"

"Because I don't watch MTV!" (My daughter is like her daddy. She is honest to a fault.)

Then I recalled our previous conversation about "Not Gonna Bow." I asked her, "Do you remember that song by Russ Taff?"

"Yeah," she answered.

"Do you remember how Bobby's friends wanted him to be just like them, getting him to compromise his standards? See how that relates to how you behaved in school today? Everyone was saying, 'Come on, Ann, won't you be like us!' And you said, 'I'm not gonna bow. I'm not going to bow to that pressure.'"

When I explained the significance of what she had done, she beamed with happiness. And I was excited about teaching spiritual values to my daughter through the medium of music.

At that point I began to let her listen to as much Christian music as I could. After she listens to a new tape, I ask her questions about the issues raised in the songs. I want her to think about the spiritual significance of everything she does, and these lessons come easiest through Christian music.

I take Christian music whenever we travel. Why listen to secular music when there is so much great Christian music to listen to? If I'm driving with one of my daughters, I always try to take along at least one tape with the spiritual values I'd like to communicate at that time. I also take one of her favorites, just in case she doesn't want to listen to mine. I might put on the first tape under the pretext that it's merely entertainment. But when it comes to a significant lyric, I ask, "Did you hear that?" I wait for her to respond yes or no. If she says no, I rewind it so she can hear it again. Then I ask her what it means.

To be honest, sometimes this approach works and sometimes it doesn't. If she isn't interested in a long discussion, I put her favorite tape in. But my daughters and I have had some of the deepest spiritual discussions about honesty, love, spiritual values, and the Christian life—all because music introduced the subject and we were able to discuss it right then and there.

INNOCENCE AND REDEMPTION

One time we were listening to a song by Margaret Becker titled "Streets of Innocence" from her album *The Reckoning.* In the song, Margaret speaks of the joy of being morally innocent and reveals that her friends are often unable to sleep at night because they have compromised their values and principles. She sings, "You can have your money, you can have your fame, but I've got innocence and I can sleep at night."

When the song was through, my younger daughter Allison asked, "Daddy, what does 'innocence' mean?"

What a joy it was to share with her. I said, "Honey, you're innocent because you don't know how much pain sin can bring into your life. I can't really explain to you what it's like not to be innocent. But it's my prayer that you will remain innocent of sin and greed your whole life." Because of that song I was able to talk to her (for quite some time) about how God has made us innocent and how sin can wipe away that precious innocence.

Under normal circumstances, if I were to tell my daughter I wanted to talk to her about innocence, she would have a hard time sitting still. But because it was a topic *she* brought up, she sat in rapt attention as we discussed what was on her mind.

At another time, when Ann was 11, she and I were listening to Kim Boyce's *Time and Again* album. This album contains a song called "Not for Me." I asked, "Do you understand what Kim is saying?"

She proceeded to explain it in detail. In the song Kim describes being tempted to go out with a non-Christian guy, but she decided against it because it could weaken her testimony and ruin her moral commitment. Even though she liked the guy, she decided not to see him.

After Ann thought for a while she asked, "Daddy, what's so wrong about going out with non-Christian guys? I don't plan on marrying one. But if I just want to go out on a date, non-Christian guys can be fun, too."

Here was an 11-year-old girl with a valid question, even though she wouldn't be dating for five more years. (We had already discussed the dating issue. I wanted her to wait until she was 37, but we compromised on 16.) I took advantage of this opportunity for a long discussion of such an important matter. It was made much easier through the message of a Christian song.

Every once in a while, we hear of other families who are able to discuss important spiritual issues prompted by Christian music. For example, a few years back, a father phoned my office one day asking for advice. He had a son who was slightly retarded and somewhat disabled, making it difficult for him to fit in with other boys his age. The father tried to help him feel comfortable with his friends as best he could.

The son had told his dad that many of his friends listened to Bon Jovi, and the father was wondering if it was okay to purchase the music of that group for his son. We wouldn't recommend the sex-and-party mentality of this popular pop metal group, but we suggested that he substitute a particular Christian group that had the same kind of sound, but with a solid Christian message.

The father bought the tape we suggested and gave it to his son. The boy loved it. In fact, he took it with him to a weekend Boy Scout camp. When the other boys started to put Bon Jovi into their tape player, this young man said, "Hey, I have a better tape. Let's listen to this. It's a Christian group and they're better than Bon Jovi."

"No way!" his buddies retorted.

"Yeah, it's true," said the boy. "Check this out."

They listened to it and they all really liked it. The Christian tape was a big hit all weekend.

As he was driving home from camp with his father, the young man went on and on about how neat the Christian rock band was and how the kids thought he was cool because of his tape. But the real turning point for the father was when his son turned and asked, "Dad, one of the songs on the tape talks about 'redemption.' What does that mean?"

For 45 minutes, that father was able to explain the gospel to his 14-year-old son and talk with him about his faith in Jesus Christ. He called us later, ecstatic, wondering if there were other groups he could encourage his son with.

SOME MUSIC DILEMMAS

Raising children is not all clichés and easy answers. More than once, I've had my theories about music put to the test. One time Ann asked if she could have a certain album by a relatively innocent secular performer. She had heard it at a girlfriend's house. I was not naive enough to think that she would never listen to secular music, but I was a little disappointed that she wanted to own this tape. She already had dozens of Christian tapes, including some that sounded very much like the secular artist she was asking for. What should I do? You would think if anyone had the answers, it would be me, right? Wrong. I was stumped, so I prayed for wisdom.

This was a situation where it would be a lot easier to think for the child than to challenge her to think for herself. As Ann's father, I had every right to tell her that I didn't want anything but Christian music in my house. But I didn't want to take the easy way out by making a decision without considering her.

We *do* have a rule in our home to avoid music which is against biblical values. But this artist didn't oppose biblical values. She was simply empty, not evil. After much prayer and thought, I decided to challenge Ann to think through the situation and make her own decision. We sat down and I asked some questions: *Why did she want this album when she knew I would not approve? Why did she want an album that looked at life from a perspective that left God out? Why did she want a non-Christian album when she already had so many good Christian ones?*

As we talked, I realized I could never keep her from every influence of the world. I told her that my desire was to give her the strength to handle these situations on her own. The day will come when I no longer have control over her actions. If I don't teach her to think for herself now, how is she ever going to learn how to think when I'm not around?

I decided not to buy that album for her because I didn't believe it would be in her best interest. But I told her if she really wanted the album, she could buy it on her own. I also reminded her that I would buy any Christian album she wanted. I *did* find a new one that was very similar to the secular artist she liked. We listened to it together and discussed what she could learn from it.

Eventually, she decided she didn't want the secular album badly enough to spend her own money. In fact, her friend ended up buying the same Christian album I had purchased for Ann. My daughter had shared it with her and they both liked it better.

To be honest, I'm still not sure whether Ann changed her mind to please her daddy, because she really changed her attitude, or because she's cheap. All I know for sure is that she is still willing to discuss these things with me. I pray that will always be true.

By now my daughters have received dozens of Christian music tapes from their mom and me. Through the years they have enjoyed music from Kids Praise to Keith Green, from Steve Taylor to Petra. And today their favorites include DC Talk, Jars of Clay, and MXPX. But one day Ann wanted a Christian rock tape that I felt was too extreme for her tastes. I believed that some aspects of the group's appearance were unbecoming for Christians.

In the past when Ann asked to listen to music or see movies and TV programs that weren't appropriate, I explained my reasons and she had always understood. But this time after I explained my concerns about this group, she still wanted the tape. What should I do?

I didn't want to lose all communication with my independent-thinking daughter by insisting I was right. After all, I had always told her she could have any Christian tape she wanted. And this case wasn't a clear matter of right or wrong. It was a gray issue. But if I gave into Ann's wishes this time, would it be the beginning of more and more compromises? I thought being a parent was going to be easier than this!

I had already evaluated the tape by God's standards in Scripture and found no problem with the lyrics. They were spiritual and biblical. Nor could I argue that God wouldn't approve of the sound. I suspected that He might not approve of the group's appearance, but could I throw out the tape because I didn't approve of their appearance?

I couldn't see anything wrong with this band for a young person already into this type of music. But my daughter was naive to this aggressive sound. I felt that a group like this might be too much for her. My biggest question was whether God would use this music in the life of my daughter.

It was at this point that my views on Christian music and Christian parenting came into conflict. The daddy in me still didn't want Ann to listen to this tape. I want my daughter to listen to Christian music that helps her focus on life from God's viewpoint. But as her parent, it's my responsibility to set guidelines for her. I challenged myself to pray and think this through.

I finally decided to give her the tape without the cover. She would have the music she wanted without being exposed to the group's appearance. It was a subtle reminder that I had reservations about the album. I also challenged her to evaluate her decision. Did she really want this album for ministry, enjoyment, or because I didn't want her to have it? She listened to the tape once or twice and put it aside. She hasn't listened to it since.

Now, for the record, this tape that caused me so much concern was the same one that had been so popular with the young Boy Scout and his friends at camp— the tape which had opened up a warm and fruitful conversation between that boy and his father concerning redemption in Jesus Christ our Lord.

I was certainly reminded that different spices can enhance the meat of God's Word in different ways. What is suitable for one Christian's tastes may not be appropriate for another. And though I am responsible for my daughter's spiritual growth, I must be careful not to suppose that I always know what will minister to her.

I'm just glad there's so much good Christian music available to strengthen our spiritual walks. I'd like to challenge every Christian to use Christian music to revitalize his faith and joy in Jesus Christ. ⫴

Chapter 16

THE CHRISTIAN MUSIC DIET

●

*"We take captive every thought to make it
obedient to Christ." (2 Corinthians 10:5)*

I listened intently to the young man who was pouring out his fears and frustrations to me. "Every time I try to pray or read my Bible, wicked, sexual thoughts spring into my mind. I can't get rid of them, no matter how hard I try. It's frustrating. A Christian shouldn't have these thoughts. If I'm a Christian, I should be more like Christ."

Pat was a new Christian, one of several young marines who attended the Sunday school class I taught. He had asked to talk with me in private, where he began to describe his troubles. Before he had become a Christian, these thoughts hadn't particularly bothered him. But now they had him completely discouraged.

"What kind of music do you listen to?" I asked.

"Why?" Pat asked, a puzzled look on his face. "My music is not the problem. It's my thought life."

"Actually, you're struggling with your faith in Jesus and the joy of your salvation," I told him.

We read Colossians 2:8 together. Then I suggested, "Since most rock music is based on thoughts and ideas that are against what Jesus taught, we need to look at the philosophies of the music you listen to." As we discussed Pat's listening habits, it became quite clear that they were having a negative effect on his thought life. His thoughts, in turn, were stifling his faith and joy about being a Christian.

I suggested that Pat put aside his sexual secular music for a while and substitute Christian music to see if the change would have any effect on his thought life. Sure enough, within a few weeks of changing his listening habits, Pat's entire demeanor changed. Over a period of time, we could see a positive attitude toward spiritual things develop in his life. His faith was growing. He began to view life from God's perspective instead of man's. The joy of his salvation returned. God was in the process of healing Pat's mind. Bible study, prayer, and Christian fellowship also became important elements of his renewal process.

"Why should I listen to music that will drag me down," Pat reasoned, "when I can listen to music that will heal instead?" Exactly! Today Pat is a seminary graduate and pastor of a growing church in the Chicago area.

A CHALLENGE TO OUR FAITH

It was becoming more and more obvious to me that many Christians needed a radical change in their musical habits if they were going to grow in Christ. At best, the secular music so many Christians listen to is Twinkie music—empty calories with no nutritional value. At worst, it can be absolute poison to their souls. That's why so many of them have such a difficult time spiritually, emotionally, mentally, and morally. The music they feed on doesn't give them the strength they need to resist temptation, restore their faith and joy, and build strong spiritual muscles to experience victory in Christ.

Pat was one of the first people I ever challenged to change his musical diet. Eventually the challenge evolved into the 30-Day Christian Music Diet. It is a simple plan to change a person's thought life and deepen faith and joy in Jesus Christ by focusing exclusively on Christian music and media for a specific period of time.

We encourage all Christians to put away their secular entertainment and consume nothing but musical steak (Christian music) for 30 days. They should put away their secular CDs, cassettes, and videos. They should also switch off the TV, except for occasional newscasts they know won't conflict with biblical values.

How about you? Are you ready to take this challenge? If so, the easiest way to execute the plan is to get some Christian music cassettes to play in your car's tape deck or at home. If you can't find enough Christian music, then listen to teaching tapes from Christian speakers, read the Bible or Christian books, talk to your friends, talk to the Lord, or minister to the people around you. Plan your leisure hours to accomplish Christian purposes.

Completely surrender all your entertainment to the Lord. Fill your mind with the thoughts of Christ through Christian music. At the end of 30 days, evaluate your spiritual life. How do you feel? How's your faith and joy in Christ? How's your thought life? Do you notice any significant changes in your attitudes and/or behaviors? Do your friends see a difference in you? After your evaluation, you can return to what you used to listen to. But it is my contention that you will experience a noticeable change. Many people who start on this strict Christian music diet never go back to their old forms of entertainment.

If it doesn't do anything else, the 30-Day Christian Music Diet will create a gauge to help you measure your slavery to the world and your faith in Christ. I gave this challenge at a Christian youth convention, and many of the attendees decided to accept the challenge. But one young man came up to me in a panic. He acted like someone going through drug withdrawal, wringing his hands and complaining nervously. He told me, "It's been hard enough going without my music for the past 2 days. I know I can't make it for *30* days!"

What was he revealing about his faith? Although he wanted to get right with God, he was beginning to see that he was a slave to his music. Someone has said that if you have something you can't give away, you don't own it. It owns you.

Your ability to stick to the Christian Music Diet is an immediate measure of your attachment to the world. If the discipline to stay away from secular music does not come easily, it's a clue as to how much the music has a hold of your life. Everyone says they can take or leave something—until they actually have to leave it! It's like the guy who claims he can quit smoking any time. To prove it, he quit ten times just last week!

Entertainment can become a gauge that determines whether we are *in* the world or *of* the world. Are we moving through life directed by Christ, or does the world have its grip on us? We can't assume that just because we received Christ years ago we will never fall under the influence of the world again. Whether teenagers, parents, or grandparents, we need to examine our lives regularly to see if the world has gained a hold on any part of our lives. Many Christians don't realize how dependent they are on the things of the world until they try to remove those influences from their lives.

The Christian Music Diet will also provide you with a yardstick to measure your faith in Christ. Too many people approach Christianity living as close to the edge as possible. It is a contest to see how much they can get away with. How far can they go before it's really sin?

We tend to believe that if there is nothing wrong with doing a certain thing, it must be right. But we should be asking, "How close can I come to Jesus Christ?" Anything that gets in the way must be set aside. Then our attitude becomes, "How far can I go to honor my Lord Jesus Christ?" We are no longer concerned with what's the least offensive thing a Christian can do, but rather the most holy thing a Christian can strive for.

Let's look at Paul's example. In Philippians 3, he makes a long list of his accomplishments, but immediately deems them all worthless compared to Christ and the power of His resurrection. He states over and over that he has not yet reached the place where he wants to be. And then he hits us with the zinger: "All of us who are mature should take such a view of things" (Philippians 3:15).

Here is Paul, one of the spiritual giants in the Bible, saying that a sign of maturity is admitting that you are in a continual process of growth. Your church may be a good one, and you may not be experiencing many problems in your personal life, but are these signs that your Christian life is all it could be? It's easy to mistake comfort for faith, or lack of trouble for God's blessing. Paul admonishes us to measure our faith by the fire of our commitment, not by how comfortable we are.

The best reason to participate in a 30-Day Christian Music Diet is because it conforms to biblical guidelines. Paul tells us to take every thought captive for Jesus Christ (2 Corinthians 10:5), which means we should consciously make an effort to monitor what goes into our brains. If we would prayerfully evaluate our entertainment to see how much it honors the Lord, we would find that many of the things we watch and listen to don't qualify.

DIETS DON'T WORK?

The average person today knows a lot about diets and the desire to lose weight. Who can avoid hearing about the Slim-Fast Diet, the Weight Watcher's Diet, the Jenny Craig diet, and all the others? I frequently run into someone who claims to have tried them all, complaining that they just don't work. But that's not really true. Diets *do* work. Somewhere along the line, the failure to accomplish the desired goal rests on the person, not the diet.

Some people have the same skepticism about the 30-Day Christian Music Diet. They ask, "Can't I listen to a little bit of secular music as long as I listen to mostly Christian music?" (In other words, "How much can I get away with?") I always respond with a question of my own: How many cookies does it take to ruin a diet? Then I illustrate the question with a personal story.

My mother-in-law, who is a wonderful cook, inevitably goes on a cooking binge just when I start a diet. Last time this happened, she was trying a new recipe for chocolate chip cookies—giant, soft, munchy, dripping, ready-to-melt-in-your-mouth chocolate chip cookies with an aroma that could make a strong man cry.

After I had completed a few successful days of my diet, Mom offered me one of her incredible edibles just out of the oven. "Al," she said, "I've just been doing a little baking. This is a new recipe. Try one."

I put up my hands. "Oh, I can't," I objected. "I just started a diet and chocolate chip cookies are definitely not on it."

"But I just baked them fresh for you and the girls," she said. "They're really good. Surely *one* won't spoil your diet."

I looked meekly at the plate of goodies and then at the face of my mother-in-law. She would be hurt and insulted if I didn't try one. And she was right—one cookie couldn't destroy my diet. "I'll have just one," I said bravely as I reached out for the sugary delight.

I had hardly enough time to enjoy the cookie before guilt set in. I realized with a pang of regret that I had just failed in my good intentions and had added fat to my body. In a panic, I ran to the scale in the bathroom and peered at the dial to determine how many pounds I had put on. It was amazing! The dial showed that I had gained no weight at all!

I felt better at once. I returned to the kitchen and was met by my mother-in-law with a plate in her hand. "Al," she said, "there are just two cookies left. Why not finish them off?"

Since I hadn't gained any weight from one cookie, I said, "Well, I guess I could." I snapped up both cookies and gobbled them down. Feeling guilty again, I ran back to the scales. Whew! I still hadn't gained any weight. Maybe I would be able to balance my diet with some of the things I like to eat.

But by then the floodgates had been opened. Soon I was not only eating cookies, but sampling my mother-in-law's German chocolate cake as well. Then I had some of her cherry pie. Before long I was eating pizza, Twinkies, and everything else in the kitchen. Snort, snort, grunt, grunt! I had become a pig back at the trough and my diet was ruined.

I'm exaggerating just a little bit, but you get the point. How many cookies does it take to ruin a diet? Just one. The first one. It's not that one cookie alone destroys a diet, but it opens the door to accept all kinds of things that will. Only a strict diet works.

The same thing is true of a Christian music diet. Can't we just listen to a couple of secular albums or songs? No, because it only takes one musical Twinkie to counteract all the good that we are doing. Does the diet have to last an entire month? Yes, because it will take at least that long to establish the habit and start being healthy again.

Some people believe they can just stop listening to the "bad" music. Rather than trying a complete Christian music diet, they suggest they can turn off the radio or skip any songs on their tapes and albums that are "bad." But this doesn't work for at least three reasons:

1. *Such a system is impractical.* Our music is usually just background accompaniment to other activities. We can't be turning the radio on and off, guessing how long the songs and commercials are. We're not going to keep interrupting other activities to skip a track on a CD, or to fast-forward a tape. This system actually requires more discipline than it does to follow the diet.

2. *We may not be able to determine what constitutes a "bad" song.* We may have conformed so much to the world's value system that we are now entertaining ourselves with material that used to offend us. We no longer understand what is good in God's sight. If our faith and joy are suffering and we are spiritually out of shape, how perceptive can we be about what offends a most Holy God?

3. *The "bad" songs aren't the problem.* If we had the spiritual discernment and discipline to stay away from the things that are spoiling our spiritual health, we'd already be doing it! Telling someone who is struggling with faith and joy to turn off their bad music is like telling someone who is overweight to stop eating fattening foods. It just doesn't work.

Dieters need to know what foods are fattening and what foods are right for them. Then they need a plan to get to their desired weight. They need a strict plan to follow. As long as they follow the plan, they need to put very little thought into the process. There is no longer any debate as to what they can get away with. I am suggesting the same kind of strict plan with the Christian Music Diet. Every compromise and excuse is a potential source of failure.

It's important to understand that no one at Al Menconi Ministries ever says that it's impossible to listen to secular music and still be a devoted Christian. We're not advocating hiding in the Christian media so the world will go away and not bother you anymore. We're not encouraging Christians to stick their heads in the sand and pretend the world doesn't exist. We know the world is out there. Christians are called to be in the world but not of it. However, many think they are not worldly, when actually the world has a strong grip on their lives. We hope to help strengthen their faith and joy so they can effectively minister in the world without being overtaken by its philosophies.

Nor have we ever said that eliminating secular music from your life will automatically make you spiritual. What we are saying is that you probably don't understand how much control the entertainment media has over you. And you will never fully understand until you completely step away from it. Of course, some people can listen to Christian music until they are blue in the face and it won't make any difference. The 30-day diet will only work for an individual who wants to serve Jesus and who wants to do what's best for a strong spiritual life.

SOME CASE HISTORIES

Tracy was probably the most rebellious girl in our Christian high school. She claimed to be a Christian, but once she told me in a counseling session, "Sometimes I even hate the name 'Christian.' It has been pushed down my throat since I was four."

Tracy was asked to leave school after her sophomore year because of her involvement with drugs. I didn't know or understand the full extent of Tracy's problems, but she wanted nothing to do with authority, Christianity, or further education. After leaving behind all church involvement and frequently running away from home, she finally awoke to her emptiness. She mistakenly thought she was pregnant and then saw how quickly her boyfriend wanted nothing to do with her. Tracy came face-to-face with the reality of a life without Jesus. At the age of 16, she could think of nothing worth living for.

But instead of committing suicide, she committed her life to Jesus. She became a new and different person inside. She petitioned the school to let her return and complete her senior year. On campus, Tracy became a dynamo for Jesus. And thanks to her, I have at least one positive story to relate from the record burning I described in the opening chapter.

In my counseling sessions with her, I didn't identify music as a major negative influence in her life, but she did. Tracy was one student who burned her rock albums and didn't replace them. She testified in chapel that her old music had been a continual reinforcement of a rebellious lifestyle. In fact, burning her music collection had allowed her to at last find the peace she had been seeking all her life. On her own, she had started a Christian music diet that helped her refocus her life on Christ.

Not long ago I was in the San Francisco area where a young man in his mid-20s approached me. He said, "You don't know me, but I was a student at Moody Bible Institute when you spoke there a few years ago. I took your challenge to go on a 30-Day Christian Music Diet because my faith and my joy weren't everything I wanted them to be. I knew something was wrong; I was just 'hanging on' spiritually. During the 30 days, if I couldn't find Christian music or entertainment, I turned everything off and sat quietly. I used that time to pray and meditate on the things of God, and I developed a new love for Jesus Christ. When I graduated from college, I became a youth pastor. I was just going through the motions before, but now I have a deep love for my Lord."

The young man motioned toward a group of high-school students. "Do you see all these young people?" he asked. "They are members of my youth group and I want to introduce them to you. They have also taken on the challenge to go on a 30-Day Christian Music Diet! I can already see spiritual growth in many of them. It's all because you came to my college years ago and challenged us to go on a regular diet for the spiritual nourishment of our souls!"

THE CHALLENGE

Victory is possible in our lives and ministries, but not all of us are experiencing it. How about you? Perhaps you are one of many who will read this book, protesting at various points along the way: *"Oh, that isn't for me,"* or, *"But you don't understand,"* or, *"Really, I don't listen to the words,"* or, *"The music doesn't have a hold on my life,"* or, *"I'm a nice person."* Most of us tell ourselves all kinds of deceptive messages.

But right now, I would challenge you to honestly evaluate your faith and joy in Jesus Christ. Think back to your first encounter with Him, to the excitement and fervor you had when you became a Christian. You saw the world with such different eyes! Your mind and heart yearned for the things of God. Since those days, perhaps you have settled into a more apathetic, placid, inactive Christianity. Maybe you are going through the motions because they are now a habit, rather than being motivated by the Spirit's fire.

I strongly encourage you to try the 30-Day Christian Music Diet—not because I think it's a magic formula nor because I think I have the right to climb into your soul to tell you what ministers to you. Rather, I urge you to renew your first love. I want your faith and joy to be all it can be, and for you to have the passion for Christ you once had. I challenge you to move forward for Christ and become one of His warriors—not just a hearer of God's Word, but a doer also. And after you have done this and discovered what a difference it can make in your life, I pray that you will grow closer to your children by seeing that music is, indeed, a window to their souls.

Epilogue

After reading this book, some may wonder, "Okay, Al, so what happens in your life after chapter two?"

Al continued to teach and counsel at the same Christian high school for a few years. He also renewed his commitment to reaching parents and young people with his new, commonsense approach to music and entertainment.

But this part-time, on-the-side ministry was requiring more and more of his time. He would teach during the week, conduct local seminars in the evenings, and travel out of town for more seminars on the weekends. This was obviously not conducive to a fulfilling family life.

So in the fall of 1982, Al sent a letter to everyone he knew on a first-name basis to let them know he was going to start a full-time ministry. He is fond of saying that both people responded, "Go for it!" Actually, he contacted about 300 friends with a small letter called *Media Update*. (Today, *Media Update* is our regular newsletter read by thousands of people in all fifty states and over twenty foreign countries.)

Next, Al assembled a Board of Trustees to guide and direct his ministry. He looked for two things in board members: (1) Insights they could offer the ministry relating to their specialties (CPAs, business owners, pastors, and so forth), and (2) "No" men, as opposed to "Yes" men. Al wanted people who would think, question, and challenge his ideas (Proverbs 27:17). I believe this is one of the most important factors in the growth of the ministry.

Since the formation of Al Menconi Ministries, Al's reputation as a speaker has grown enormously. He addresses nearly 50,000 people in seminars all over the

United States and Canada each year. We have added additional speakers to our staff to try to meet the demand.

We also publish numerous resources designed to educate and encourage Christians to evaluate their music and entertainment in the light of God's Word. These resources have been in the form of audio and video teaching tapes, curriculum, books, booklets, and our bimonthly publication, *Media Update.*

Like any ministry, we have had our ups and downs. We like to innovate, not emulate, and we feel we are breaking new ground. Nobody has done what we are doing to the same extent. I appreciate the way one Kentucky mother put it: "I like your positive, loving approach that utilizes God-given creativity and wisdom. It helps us as parents approach the subject of choices of music with some degree of knowledge and wisdom. It's sort of like you made the first tracks in the heavy snow, making it easier for us to walk the road."

The Lord has been faithful in working through this ministry (sometimes in spite of ourselves). He has strengthened our work with parents and Christian leaders, helping them to effectively communicate their concerns about today's music to today's young person. He has also blessed our work with young people, exposing the truth about their music and encouraging a deeper commitment to Jesus.

If you would like more information about our ministry (seminars, resources, etc.), please feel free to contact us at Al Menconi Ministries, P.O. Box 5008, San Marcos, CA 92069. Our phone number is 619-591-4696.

Mike Atkinson
Executive Director
Al Menconi Ministries

130/85

160/90